A. Philip Randolph

and the

African-American

Labor Movement

A. Philip Randolph

and the African-American Labor Movement

Calvin Craig Miller

**MORGAN
REYNOLDS**
Publishing, Inc.

620 South Elm Street, Suite 223
Greensboro, North Carolina   27406
http://www.morganreynolds.com

Portraits of Black Americans

Bayard Rustin
A. Philip Randolph
Roy Wilkins
W. E. B. Du Bois
Gwendolyn Brooks
Marcus Garvey
William Grant Still
Richard Wright
Thurgood Marshall
Langston Hughes
John Coltrane

A. PHILIP RANDOLPH AND THE AFRICAN-AMERICAN LABOR MOVEMENT

Library of Congress Cataloging-in-Publication Data

Miller, Calvin Craig, 1954-
  A. Philip Randolph and the African American labor movement / Calvin Craig Miller.— 1st ed.
    p. cm.
  Includes bibliographical references and index.
  ISBN 1-931798-50-8 (alk. paper)
  1. Randolph, A. Philip (Asa Philip), 1889- 2. African Americans—Biography. 3. Civil rights workers—United States—Biography. 4. African Americans—Civil rights—History—20th century. 5. Civil rights movements—United States—History—20th century. 6. Brotherhood of Sleeping Car Porters—History. 7. Labor unions—United States—History—20th century. I. Title.
  E185.97.R27M55 2003
  323'.092—dc22

2004023706

Printed in the United States of America
First Edition

Contents

One

Pride Against Prejudice

Asa Philip Randolph was about ten when a group of solemn, angry men arrived at his Jacksonville, Florida, home one afternoon. They wanted to see his father, Reverend James William Randolph. The reverend gathered the men in the family's sparse living room, and they told him what had happened.

A black man had been locked up in the Duval County jail and angry white men were muttering about hanging him without a trial. Such hangings, known as lynchings, were terribly familiar to black people, particularly in the South. But the city of Jacksonville had a tradition of African-American pride; the black men gathered in the Randolph house were not willing to tolerate a lynching. Guns packed, they were prepared to encircle the jail and

Opposite: A. Philip Randolph. *(National Portrait Gallery, Washington, D.C.)*

greet the white mob with force. They wanted the reverend to join them.

The Randolphs kept two guns in the house, a Bulldog pistol and a shotgun. James Randolph handed his wife the shotgun, took the Bulldog for himself and headed for the jail. Elizabeth Randolph, a dead shot, kept the gun cradled across her lap for the rest of the night. The reverend returned home at dawn, exhausted but relieved. When the lynch mob was confronted with the jail's armed defenders they had wisely backed down.

Asa Randolph remembered that day for the rest of his life. He had seen plenty of violence and racial hatred before, but this was the first time he had seen black Americans take up arms against bigotry. It filled him with pride.

Asa had grown up on the rough side of Jacksonville. He and his older brother James had received a good education in the city's schools, but they had to learn to fight as well. Street bullies resented their success in school, and as they were growing up, the once-tolerant community of Jacksonville became increasingly more oppressive toward its black citizens.

When Asa's father, the Reverend James William Randolph, came to Jacksonville in 1891 to take over the congregation of a small African-American Episcopal church, Jacksonville seemed to be a welcoming place, especially when compared to the prevailing southern prejudice against African Americans. Black policemen patrolled the streets and firehouses sent out black

While Jacksonville was traditionally a tolerant city, the trend throughout the South toward an increasingly segregated society eventually penetrated the community. Segregated public facilities, such as the Jacksonville train station pictured here, became more common during Asa's childhood.

firefighters. African Americans served as judges and members of the city council. A black man could get his hair cut in the same barbershop as whites.

Jacksonville seemed worlds apart from the community of Monticello, Virginia, where Asa's father had grown up. James Randolph, born in 1864, was the descendant of slaves owned by the well-respected Randolph family. Many whites in Monticello resented blacks, most of whom had lived as slaves until the end of the Civil War in 1865. African Americans in Monticello carried firearms to protect themselves.

Former slaves in most areas of the South in the years after the Civil War had to feel their way carefully. They lived in a region of plantation owners that had recently been allowed to take their labor for no wages, enforce discipline with guns and whips, and chase them down with dogs if they tried to escape.

But African Americans in Monticello created a resistance to racism that was rare for its time and militant in nature, even to the point of taking up arms to preserve blacks' right to vote. When rumors of death threats against blacks spread during one particularly violent year, angry black activists responded by nailing a note to the door of the post office: "We understand that the White People in This Place Say they intend to Kill some of the Colored People in This Place. If such a thing is started Here We Would Not give much for this Place Town and People." James grew up admiring people who were willing to stand up and fight against racial oppression. This was a trait he passed on to his two sons.

James attended a school set up by Methodist missionaries for the children of former slaves. He loved learning and excelled at his bookwork. James decided he wanted to be a preacher, a high calling for young black men at the time. In his teens he became a Sunday school teacher for the African Methodist Episcopal (AME) church.

James Robinson, a family friend, helped James Randolph get his first ministry in Baldwin, Florida. He had made the acquaintance of the four Robinson daughters: Mattie, Esther, Carrie, and Elizabeth. Just before James Randolph was ordained a minister, the Robinsons moved to Baldwin, a town in northeast Florida about fifteen miles from Jacksonville. The Robinsons did not like the Baldwin AME church as much as they had liked the one in Monticello. They thought that young James Randolph, still without a pulpit of his own, could preach better sermons, and persuaded other members of the congregation to join them in extending an offer. James arrived in Baldwin in 1884.

Baldwin was a poor and rugged little lumber town with unnamed dirt streets, occupied by about four hundred mostly working-class residents. They made their livings cutting pulpwood, dipping turpentine, and cutting wood trestles for railroad tracks. James's first church was equally humble, a small wooden chapel at the intersection of two unpaved roads. He preached to a congregation of about fifty people, under kerosene lamps strung from the rafters. He frequently stayed at the Robinson's log cabin, a house so drafty that the family had to stuff newspapers in the walls to keep out the cold winter wind. At night he could see the stars through the cracks in the roof.

The brightest student in his Sunday school class was the youngest of the Robinson daughters, Elizabeth. James began courting her and in 1885 they married. James was twenty-one, his bride just thirteen. Elizabeth bore their first son, James, two years later in May of 1887. Shortly thereafter they moved to Crescent City, where Asa Philip Randolph was born on April 15, 1889. Asa was named after an Old Testament king who gave away royal riches to his servants.

After a little more than two years in Crescent City, the Reverend Randolph received an invitation to take over a church in Jacksonville. The offer, from a church with about thirty members, did not bring much in the way of prestige or great income. But the reverend saw some advantages in taking the position. The Jacksonville church would allow him to lead services in other churches as well, including the one in Baldwin. Furthermore, he saw moving to a larger town as a step up for the family.

Jacksonville had no rules or laws requiring segregation—not even the prohibitions against the mixing of the races in public that were so rigorously enforced in many southern towns and cities. Well-to-do black people lived in some of the best homes in the city and rode in fine carriages.

Not all African Americans, of course, belonged to the upper classes. Reverend Randolph's congregations were filled with the poor and working class, and his collection plates did not overflow like those of the churches where the wealthy worshipped. But he had not chosen his profession to seek wealth. In fact, he seemed almost indifferent to matters of making money, a trait that Asa would inherit. Principle was more important, and Asa would adopt that philosophy as well.

As Asa and his brother James grew up, the family suffered frequent financial hardships. They lived in a house with green weatherboard siding, a shingled roof, and a picket fence in such poor repair that dogs and cats wandered through the broken slats. Elizabeth Randolph worked hard to keep the house clean, scrubbing and waxing the floors to a bright shine every Saturday. The most ornate item in the living room was a kerosene lamp with a fancy flowered shade. A fireplace heated the living room, while any warmth upstairs came from an iron stove.

Asa's beloved older brother, James Randolph.

The Reverend Randolph was tall and thin, with a deep, powerful voice that carried well into the back pews. Asa recalled his father as having "a nose, a chin beard, and a certain refinement and polish of bearing." He carried himself proudly, with his shoulders held back, and taught his boys to do the same. He said that people who slumped when they walked showed that they did not respect themselves very much. Elizabeth Randolph was also tall, with light skin and beautiful long hair. Her life centered on the church; she had few friends outside it. She would hold her face in her hands and weep after testifying to her faith during a service.

Elizabeth managed both the two boys' discipline and the household finances. She did not hesitate to thrash the boys when they misbehaved. The worst they endured from their father was a scolding, for he could never bring himself to strike them.

James Randolph was a man of high principles, but did not have much business sense. Money was always an afterthought. When collection plates ran low, he was reluctant to press church leaders for payment. "If the church paid him, okay; if it didn't, okay too," recalled one of his wife's nieces. "His wife was the go-getter." To Elizabeth's dismay, he stretched the family budget thinner by slipping the boys money behind her back.

James did manage to raise enough money to buy a plot of land at the corner of Eighth and Davis streets. There he built his first church in Jacksonville, the New Hope AME Chapel. He also took on occasional preaching duties in Palatka and Green Cove Springs. But work in the pulpit did not bring great financial rewards. The boys would watch as their father counted out a salary gleaned from collection plates of the poor congregations. There were no bills, only coins, none larger than a quarter. Sometimes Reverend Randolph carried his pay home on his back in a burlap sack—fruit, corn, potatoes, and perhaps a side of pork in place of money.

Poor churches "allowed" their pastors to work jobs during the week, a necessary arrangement because they could not have survived otherwise. James Randolph attempted several businesses, none successfully. Using skills he had learned in Monticello, he opened a tailor's shop in the backyard, where he and Elizabeth altered and dyed clothes. In the beginning, most of their customers took their services on credit, which they almost never paid. Elizabeth put a stop to the practice, implementing a policy of "no cash, no clothes." Even with her no-nonsense policy, the business made a meager profit of about ten dollars a week. In a bad week, the Randolphs might make no more than three dollars.

The tailor shop's modest success was the most the family ever achieved in business. The reverend tried other businesses. He bought a meat market, financed by an owner who had gone bankrupt. It failed within a month, leaving the Randolphs saddled with debt. Then James Randolph started a business buying wood at wholesale and hiring a man to sell it from a cart. The idea seemed sound since many people heated their homes with wood. But once again, Randolph's business sense fell short. The cart driver skimmed from the profits, sales fell short of the break-even point, and the reverend again had to shut down.

Reverend Randolph grew weary of failing in business. One reason he failed was likely his belief that spiritual matters outweighed any earthly concerns. He counted racial justice as important and taught his sons to do the same. He taught them that many important historic figures were black, such as the general Hannibal, the rebel slave leader Nat Turner, and the abolitionist orator Frederick Douglass.

These were not the lessons the boys found in the books they read, which mainly focused on history as made by white people. Asa and James did not always agree with their father on spiritual matters, but they did adopt his sense of racial pride. When they accompanied him on his circuit preaching, he introduced them as "two of the finest boys in the world."

Jacksonville changed as the boys grew up. The racism that pervaded other areas of the South began to creep into the once-tolerant city in the early years of the twentieth century. City officials passed "Jim Crow" ordinances. Jim Crow was the name of stereotypical black characters in nineteenth-century minstrel shows and referred to laws that kept the races separated or "segregated" in public places. White restaurants could choose not to serve blacks, and public bathrooms were labeled "White" and "Colored." When they went to theatres, African Americans had to sit in the balcony.

Everyday relations with white people, once friendly, began to show ugly traces of racism. Asa and James became paperboys for the *Times-Union* newspaper. When they went to get their papers, white boys shoved them to the back of the line. Even worse, they saw their father insulted in front of them. They once accompanied him as he delivered a load of mended clothes to the white foreman of a sawmill. Far from being grateful for the delivery, the man was infuriated to see a black man at his place of business.

"Get the hell out of here," the man shouted at Rev-

This late nineteenth-century drawing of the minstrel character "Jim Crow" gives an idea of the derogatory and racist ways in which African Americans were portrayed when Asa was young.

erend Randolph. "Take the clothes to my house or I'll throw you off the property." James Randolph silently turned away, swallowing his rage, and left.

Reverend Randolph did not bear every indignity in silence. Like other black people in Jacksonville, he felt he had suffered enough abuse by the time the lynch mob formed at the Duval County jail. Their brave armed stand helped him and his family reconcile themselves to the humiliations they had to endure daily. Asa would never forget the sense of vindication that was earned by fighting injustice.

The fight, however, was one his family would have to wage time and again. Jacksonville city leaders continued to pass segregation laws that prohibited blacks and whites from mixing in public places, which included streetcars and library reading rooms. Reverend Randolph forbade his sons to use such facilities. The boys missed the libraries, but they understood that they should not cave in to racial intimidation.

The two brothers formed an alliance that helped them survive the bullying they encountered at Oakland Elementary School. James was a better student than Asa, particularly in language and mathematics. He tutored his younger brother so that he could also excel in school. Their success pleased their teachers, but not some of their duller-witted classmates. The two boys frequently faced after-school ambushes from bullies who resented their success. James fought back fiercely, even against attackers who were bigger and stronger. Asa hated having to fight, but he learned to do his part. Whenever their mother learned that her sons had been fighting, she wanted to know one thing first—had they fought back? If they had not, she would whip them, for she hated cowards.

The boys entered Cookman Institute in 1903, when Asa was fourteen. Founded by Methodists in 1872, Cookman was Florida's only high school for blacks. It offered students what the administration considered to

The Cookman Institute, where Asa and James attended high school.

be a practical mix of the higher branches of learning and occupational skills. Young African Americans could learn Greek, Latin, French, natural science, and advanced mathematics. They could also take courses in shoemaking, tailoring, printing, and agriculture. Teachers assumed those working-class skills would offer their students the best chance of making a living.

Asa had no desire to be a tailor, a shoemaker, or a farmer. He enjoyed English and literature classes the most. Mathematics frustrated him, but fortunately James was a math wizard and helped Asa with his assignments. James had always overshadowed Asa in elementary school, but at Cookman, Asa developed a reputation as a serious scholar in his own right.

Two excellent teachers helped nurture Asa's aca-

Mary Neff played a large role in Asa's success as a student at the Cookman Institute.

demic gifts. Lillie Whitney taught Greek, Latin, and mathematics, while Mary Neff instructed classes in literature, ethics, and drama. Both took notice of the Randolph brothers' intellectual talents. James became a favorite of Whitney's, while Asa blossomed in Neff's classes. Asa became one of the school's best students in public speaking, drama, and literature. "I was important in my own right," Asa said later, recalling his emergence from his brother's shadow.

Indeed, Asa began to take an interest in subjects that bored his brother. During the years he was enrolled at Cookman, two of the nation's most respected African Americans, Booker T. Washington and W. E. B. Du Bois, were engaged in a spirited debate about the role black people should play in society. Asa read every word about the debate that he could get his hands on.

Washington headed the Tuskegee Institute, a black vocational school in Tuskegee, Alabama. He believed African-American education should focus on the teaching of trades, so that the black race could become economically self-sufficient. He argued that black people were not ready for social equality so soon after the end of slavery. Washington believed that the proper place for blacks to start was the bottom of the economic ladder. He even supported segregation, a position that greatly pleased his white supporters in the South. He developed such political clout in the Republican Party that his detractors referred to his circle as "the Tuskegee Machine."

Du Bois deplored Washington's "go slow" approach

A classroom at Booker T. Washington's Tuskegee Institute in 1902. *(Library of Congress)*

One of Asa's influences, W. E. B. Du Bois. *(Library of Congress)*

to equality. In his book *The Souls of Black Folk,* he spoke of the black intellectuals, artists, and professionals as the "talented tenth," that ten percent of the black population that would help to lead it out of the slave mentality. He helped found the National Association for the Advancement of Colored People (NAACP), which waged battles for African Americans throughout the twentieth century. While Washington reaped the praise of conservative whites, Du Bois more often faced scorn as a "race radical."

Du Bois was not too radical for Asa. Though Asa initially hoped to become a stage actor, he also, like his father, wanted more than personal success. Du Bois's writing inflamed him with a desire to bring about social change for his race and inspired him all the more to learn to write and express himself more eloquently. As his graduation from Cookman neared, in 1901, Asa was named the class valedictorian. He gave a speech called

"The Man of the Hour," a title which could have described his own elation at the honor.

Asa Philip Randolph as a young man.

He did not feel quite so much like the man of the hour when he found out how little his education counted in the work world. In order to earn a living he had to take on numerous menial jobs—and detested them all. He collected insurance premiums, laid railroad ties, clerked in a grocery store, drove a delivery wagon for a drug store, and shoveled fertilizer.

Asa wanted something more out of life than back-breaking, mindless labor and a meager paycheck. He began to consider moving out of Jacksonville. During his teens, he had spent a summer vacation with a cousin who worked as a janitor in New York. While there, Asa had sold the *New York World* newspaper and helped his cousin on the job. He spent his wages on nice clothes and vaudeville shows. The city seemed like the hub of the world to the young man, a place where opportunities were almost limitless.

In April of 1911, Asa and his young friend, Beaman Hearn, made plans to sail to New York City. He told his mother he would return in the fall, but only to spare her feelings at seeing him leave. He had no intention of ever coming back to Jacksonville if he could avoid it. The two young men sailed away on the steamboat *Arapahoe*. Asa washed dishes in the ship's kitchen to help pay for his trip, taking on one more menial job in the effort to set himself free.

Two

Street Radical

When Asa Philip Randolph arrived in New York City in April of 1911, he spent a month wandering the streets of Manhattan, marveling at the sights and attending shows. In Jacksonville he had to settle for menial jobs. Here it seemed possible to achieve anything, including his dream of becoming a stage actor.

He was certainly not the only young African American to travel north with big dreams. The early years of the twentieth century saw a massive migration of blacks from the South. Many of them came from the "talented tenth" that W. E. B. Du Bois had written about: those who had grown dissatisfied with the meager livings they could eke out doing hard labor for low wages in the South. An Alabama preacher wrote to a friend in the North complaining that there were many places in the

state where "the only thing that the black man gets is a peck of meal and three to four lbs. of bacon per week, and he is treated as a slave. As leaders we are powerless for we dare not resent such or to show even the slightest signs of disapproval. Only a few days ago more than 1000 people left here for the north and west."

Another reason for the exodus was the danger that many lived under in the South, where African Americans did not get the same justice as white people. A rumor or accusation was often enough to get a black person lynched.

Many of those who headed north were bound for Harlem. But even there, friction existed between the races. White tenants and property owners had once been the largest population in Harlem, and many resented the influx of black people. But their resistance did not stop the migrants. African-American realtors, often assisted by black churches, bought up blocks of apartment buildings. Soon Harlem was the largest black neighborhood in the country, as people established a place where they could live freely and dominate the culture. The result was an African-American cultural rebirth that came to be known as the Harlem Renaissance, producing black actors, artists, writers, and political activists.

In Harlem, Randolph and his traveling companion, Beaman Hearn, had planned to stay with Randolph's aunt, but she did not have room for them. She did, however, find them lodging with a friend on 132nd Street.

Opposite: Randolph, not long after his arrival in New York City. *(Library of Congress)*

Tall and straight-shouldered, with a cultured manner of speaking, Randolph made a good first impression. The woman agreed to put them up for $1.50 a week.

After a couple of months spent under the spell of the city, attending plays and vaudeville shows, Randolph and Beaman woke up one day and realized that they did not have enough money to pay their meager rent. Their holiday was over; they had to find work. They found employment at an all-white apartment building on West 48th Street. In October, Beaman honored the promise he had made to his parents and returned to Jacksonville, where he set up a fruit and vegetable stand that he later turned into a prosperous grocery store.

Alone, Randolph struggled through a series of low-paying, menial jobs, hating them all. He worked as a porter at the Consolidated Edison Company, where he began to spend his break time buried in a book. He went on to jobs as a waiter and an elevator operator. He became adept at impressing employers in interviews, but lost jobs almost as quickly as he found them. He was still an idealist and had little patience for bosses who he thought treated workers unfairly. He worked briefly on a riverboat, living in dark cramped quarters called the glory hole. He attempted to organize the workers on board to protest living conditions and was fired for his efforts.

Randolph never took his job setbacks very seriously. His reading and his ambition to act were far more im-

Opposite: This painting by Edward Burra depicts the bustling street life of Harlem in the first decade of the twentieth century. *(Smithsonian Museum of American Art, Washington, D.C.)*

portant to him. With an open book in his hand, he would wander from one corner to another on the streets of Harlem, often reading aloud. Some people wondered if he was crazy. Everywhere he went, he would arrive with a book tucked in his back pocket.

At first, Randolph found little success in pursuing his higher ambitions. He joined a young people's Christian group, the Epworth League, not for its Biblical views but because the league sponsored a theater group. He played roles in the group's productions of Shakespeare, including plays such as *Hamlet* and *Othello*, on Sunday afternoons at the Salem Methodist Church.

One of the members of the Epworth League was a young man about Randolph's age who was going to college. At first, Randolph assumed his fellow league member was from an affluent family, since college was beyond the reach

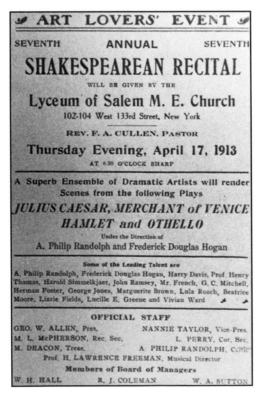

A flyer announcing the productions with which Randolph was involved through the Salem Methodist Church.

of most African Americans. But the man told him that students did not need much money to attend City College of New York. Good grades in high school were enough. Randolph hurried to enroll, and signed up for evening classes in public speaking.

There Randolph's powerful speaking voice caught the attention of Henri Strange, a leading black actor in Harlem. One day the two found themselves sharing a table at a restaurant. Strange praised Randolph's performances, and urged him to join his drama group. This might have been just the break Randolph was seeking, but for the opposition of his parents. When he wrote them in Jacksonville, they replied to say that they disapproved of the theater as an occupation. Randolph believed in honoring his parents. He declined Strange's invitation, and never again seriously considered a stage career.

Randolph now turned his energy to politics with a greater intensity than ever before. He dropped out of the Epworth League and signed up for courses in history, political science, and economics. He even formed his own political group, called the Independent Political Council. He began to center his ideas on a political and economic philosophy called socialism.

The American economy operated then, as it does now, according to the capitalist system. Under capitalism, business people and corporations set prices according to supply and demand. They can charge as much for their services and goods as buyers are willing to pay. They can also accumulate as much land and money as they can afford. At the core of the capitalist system is a belief that owning property is a fundamental right of all citizens.

Socialists seek to create a society that controls the distribution of property and income for the well-being of everyone. Goods and services go to those who need them; not just those who can afford to pay. This requires the government to control most of the economy in order to distribute equitably the goods and services. According to socialist thinkers, this economic model was the only just and fair way to run a society and to avoid wide gaps in wealth and poverty. They argued that a capitalist system worked mainly for the benefit of the wealthy.

Ironically, Randolph's skill at speaking about his radical views earned him his first chance to make money doing something he liked. In the spring of 1914, his Independent Political Council gave a presentation at Salem Methodist Church. Afterwards, a young man Randolph had known from the Epworth League, Ernest T. Welcome, came forward to congratulate him.

Welcome asked Randolph to join his fledgling employment firm. He had two goals: first, to help black migrants from the South find jobs, and second, to make money doing it. He called his company the Brotherhood of Labor. In addition to helping them find jobs, Welcome wanted to help newcomers learn the culture and social conditions prevalent in the North. He wanted Randolph to write pamphlets, both for African Americans arriving in the city and to send to those down South.

At first, Randolph was not sure about profiting from

such a good cause. He still held to his parents' belief that some goals belonged in the spiritual realm, and considered his social beliefs on the same plane. But his need for money won out and he joined the Brotherhood and began to write pamphlets.

Another stroke of luck, this one more romantic, came Randolph's way in the Brotherhood offices on 135th Street and Lenox Avenue. Down the corridor from where he worked, Lucille Green operated a prosperous beauty salon. Born in Virginia in 1883, Lucille had earned a degree at Howard University in Washington, D. C., then moved north. She had trained under Madame C. J. Walker, one of the first African-American women to become rich in business, who marketed a line of products to help black women straighten their hair. That particular cosmetic process would later fall out of fashion, but Lucille also prospered using Madame Walker's techniques. When she opened her own shop, it did a bustling business.

Lucille was five years older than Randolph, who was then twenty-five. Her hair was prematurely silver and she kept it short in the fashion of free-spirited young women of the time. She was outgoing and cheerful and loved dances and parties. Randolph had filled out as an adult and had a fuller face and strong jaw line, but he was still tall and slim—old friends still called him "String Bean."

Randolph would rather go to political meetings than dances, but Lucille brought out his fun-loving side. He did take her to political lectures during their courtship, which she enjoyed. During her university years, Lucille

Lucille Green Randolph. *(Library of Congress)*

had become a progressive on social matters and had an open mind to Asa's politics. In fact, she would later run for the New York board of aldermen as a Socialist candidate, but she also enjoyed evenings of lighter conversation and socializing at the "Dark Tower," as the mansion owned by Madame Walker's daughter A'Lelia was known. Randolph only grudgingly attended such parties, but he did enjoy taking her to plays and movies.

The couple was married in November of 1914, in St. Philip's Episcopal Church in Harlem. Randolph would have preferred a civil ceremony instead of a church wedding, but Lucille insisted. She was active in the church and thought that being married by a justice of the peace was unfit for a woman of some social standing. They had no lavish honeymoon, but instead a simple ride in an open streetcar from their Seventh Avenue apartment to South Ferry and back.

Even after their marriage, Randolph would often refuse invitations to parties, leaving Lucille to attend unescorted. At one such event, she met Chandler Owen, a friend of a friend from Howard, and a student at Columbia University. He had been born in Warrenton, North Carolina, in 1889, and had studied four years at Virginia Union University in Richmond before going on to Columbia for graduate studies. Short and stocky with piercing eyes, Owen freely offered his cynical views about society. Like Asa, he held an irreverent attitude toward established customs and institutions, but unlike Randolph, he burned with the desire to make a fortune.

Lucille thought Randolph and Owen would make a good match. She introduced the two men, and Chandler Owen became not only Randolph's best friend, but also his partner in radical political causes. No one made much money, however, preaching racial equality. Luckily for Randolph and Owen, Lucille volunteered to support both of them with her thriving business. Randolph quit his pamphlet-writing job at the Brotherhood of Labor and threw himself into his new work with Owen.

Ironically, the two young men almost fell into a financial opportunity. They made a habit of giving "soapbox speeches" on socialism and racial equality on Harlem street corners, a common practice for social reformers of the time. Orators stood on handy boxes in order to make themselves heard and visible above the crowd. William White heard some of the speeches Randolph and Owen made and liked what he heard.

White presided over the Headwaiters and Sidewaiters Society, the union for people employed in those occupations. He approached Randolph and Owen one day in 1917 as they scouted for a new office for the Independent Political Council, introduced himself, and offered them a proposition: how would the two young radicals like to become editors of a magazine?

White wanted to create a magazine to reach his union members. Randolph and Owen could choose the title and run it with complete editorial freedom. They would even have use of the society's office space. When they finished their duties with an issue, they would be free to use the office for any purpose they liked, including their political missions. The two young men could hardly believe their luck.

Randolph's close friend, Chandler Owen.

They named the magazine *The Hotel Messenger.* Working in the comfortable leather chairs and sharing a large desk with a sunny bay window facing the street, the two took a journalistic view of the waiters' problems and issues. Asa began signing his articles "A. Philip Randolph," in the manner of established New York newspaper writers who used initials in their pen names. They held meetings of the Independent Political Council in the afternoons, and their offices became a popular gathering place for those who shared their views. The situation seemed ideal.

But two such headstrong writers as Randolph and Owen turned out to be more difficult to control than White had anticipated. When a group of sidewaiters showed up one day at their office to voice a complaint, they listened with interest, regardless of the fact that the sidewaiters' anger was directed toward the headwaiters, who held the real power in the union.

The headwaiters had developed a lucrative business

apart from their main jobs, buying uniforms at wholesale prices and selling them to the sidewaiters at several times their original cost. The sidewaiters had no choice but to wear the uniforms, thus adding a considerable amount of overhead to jobs that paid little to begin with. The disgruntled employees had little difficulty persuading the editors of *The Hotel Messenger* of the injustice of their predicament and the merits of publishing a story about it. This was exactly the sort of practice the two had railed against in their street corner orations. White opened the magazine one day in 1917 to find an exposé of his own members splashed across the pages of his publication.

The headwaiters were livid and so was White. He immediately fired Randolph and Owen. The news was not a shock to the two, who knew they were daring the union's wrath. Nonetheless, they were proud of what they had written. When they left, they took the magazine with them.

They moved into two small rooms of an old Harlem brownstone. Having learned firsthand about the power of the press, Randolph and Owen were all the more determined to use it. They dropped "hotel" from the name and launched *The Messenger*. Their new magazine would transform them from street corner activists to America's "most dangerous" black men.

Three

Dangerous Men

The first issue of *The Messenger* hit newsstands in November bearing the slogan "The Only Radical Negro Magazine In America." America could not have been less prepared for a radical black magazine than it was during the winter of 1917.

The United States had entered World War I only seven months before. The war had begun in 1914 for reasons that at first seemed remote to the interests of Americans. On June 28 of that year, a Serbian terrorist assassinated Archduke Francis Ferdinand of Austria-Hungary. The assassin was part of a movement that sought to unite all Serbs into a single state. Austria-Hungary, joined by Germany, promptly declared war on Serbia.

European nations had been expecting war for years, for numerous reasons, and the assassination was the

One of the early issues of Randolph and Owen's *The Messenger*.

spark that ignited the fire. The war spread throughout Europe, drawing in one country after another. President Woodrow Wilson had initially opposed American involvement, narrowly winning reelection in 1916 with the slogan "He kept us out of war." After the election, however, when German submarines began targeting passenger ships, Wilson asked Congress for a declaration of war on Germany on April 2, 1917.

That same year another upheaval took place, one that many in the United States regarded as equally ominous. A popular revolt overthrew Czar Nicholas II of Russia. Then, a few months later, a communist group called the Bolsheviks, led by Vladimir Lenin, seized power. The Bolsheviks were proponents of a radical form of communism that saw the sort of socialism that Randolph adhered to as being as much of an enemy as was capitalism. Communists such as Lenin rejected socialism as being too gradual and too willing to find compromise with capitalism. The Bolsheviks wanted to create a communist state immediately. This insistence on rapid social transformation meant the Bolsheviks had to create a totalitarian state run by a few powerful men that had no patience for issues such as the right to free speech or to freedom of conscience.

The Messenger first appeared against this turbulent backdrop, which created distrust in many people, advocating socialism and protesting the United States' entry into the war. Before long, agents from the U.S. Department of Justice began to monitor every issue and to watch every move made by Asa Philip Randolph and Chandler Owen.

A wave of patriotism was sweeping the nation during the war, and people who spoke out against it were ostracized—or worse. The editors of *The Messenger* made clear their opposition in their first issue with an article entitled "Who Shall Pay for the War?"

The editorial demanded that "those who profit from the war should pay for it . . . How can profits be made out of the war? The answer to this question is: by selling to the government those things which are needed to keep the war going. . . . Now, Mr. Common Man, do you own any of those things? If you don't, then you cannot profit from the war. Then you ought to see to it that the government confiscates all profits made out of the war to carry on the war. Let the government take 100% and peace will come."

Randolph and Owen were particularly upset by the segregation of the military. They asked a question that few others dared at the time: why should young black men sacrifice their lives for a country that refused to let them live as equals?

In this debate, they even challenged mainstream black leaders, including Randolph's idol, W. E. B. Du Bois. Du Bois had urged African Americans to join the army and saw enlistment as a way to prove their patriotism. "We of the colored race have no ordinary interest in the outcome," he wrote in an editorial in his magazine, *The Crisis*. "That which

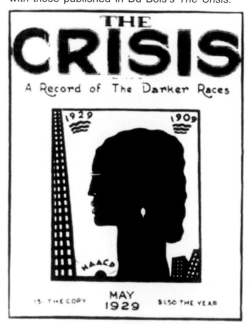

The ideas argued in *The Messenger* often clashed with those published in Du Bois's *The Crisis*.

the German power represents spells death to the aspirations of Negroes and all darker races for equality, freedom and democracy. Let us not hesitate. Let us, while this war lasts, forget our special grievances and close our ranks shoulder to shoulder with our own white fellow citizens and the allied nations that are fighting for democracy."

Du Bois's call for black sacrifice struck a sour note with Harlem radicals. In the pages of *The Messenger,* Owen fired back. "Since when has the subject race come out of a war with its rights and privileges accorded for such a participation?" he wrote. "Did not the Negro fight in the Revolutionary War, with Crispus Attucks dying first … and come out to be a miserable chattel slave in this country for nearly 100 years?"

Many African Americans were sure that if they enlisted to fight the war, they could earn more respect and equality. But letters home and reports from returning black soldiers painted a picture of an army that operated much like regular society. Black units were segregated— though they were given white commanders. Even though black units served so bravely in France that the French officers requested that the black units fight with them, American officers cautioned the French that blacks could not be trusted to fight without white supervision.

When the United States press reported the heroics of black soldiers, they often did so in the language of Jim Crow stereotypes. After African Americans spearheaded an Allied victory, a Milwaukee newspaper wrote, "Those two American colored regiments fought well, and it calls for special recognition. Is there no way of getting a cargo of watermelons over there?" Randolph and others were insulted and outraged by this kind of treatment.

Because Randolph and Owen did not support the war, and spoke out against the mistreatment of black soldiers, they frequently faced charges of being unpatriotic. But black patriots got little appreciation for their sacrifices and continued to suffer from racial violence in the very country they served. In Houston in 1917, white civilians fought black soldiers in a bloody race riot. Courts laid the blame almost entirely on the black troopers. Thirteen soldiers were condemned to hanging, another forty-one to life in prison.

Anger against the labor movement also took a disproportionate number of black lives. Randolph and Owen believed strongly in the importance of unions, but they often faced opposition from other black leaders. Du Bois, for example, urged blacks to take any jobs they could get, even as strikebreakers. People who crossed picket lines were held in contempt and called "scabs" by the strikers. Owen asked black workers to ignore Du Bois's advice, accusing him and other leaders of "preaching the gospel of hate against labor unionism, when they should be explaining to the Negroes the necessity of allying themselves with the worker's motive power and weapon—the Labor Union and the Strike."

Though Owen and Randolph had faith in the power of the union, not everyone else did. Many black people

The Messenger

Published monthly by The Messenger Publishing Co.,
513 Lenox Ave., New York City

A. PHILIP RANDOLPH,
President.

CHANDLER OWEN,
Secretary-Treasurer.

——:0:——

CONTENTS

Entered as second class mail matter at New York Post Office, N. Y., March 1917,
under the act of March 3, 1879.

The table of contents of *The Messenger* reveals the magazine's ambitious scope.

feared joining a union might cost them their jobs at a time when they had enough trouble finding jobs in the first place. When a labor conflict broke out in St. Louis and white mobs killed 125 blacks and injured hundreds more, their fears about unions were confirmed. Clearly, Randolph and Owen had staked out dangerous ground under the masthead of *The Messenger*.

Their lack of funds made their controversial publication all the more risky. While Owen talked frequently about his desire to make his fortune, he was no more successful at raising money for *The Messenger* than Randolph was. The two struggled to make ends meet, spending valuable time and energy on fund-raising lecture tours.

Fund-raising for *The Messenger* was also a dangerous proposition. Any time Randolph spoke on the magazine's main issues—opposition to the war and the need for racial equality—he put himself at risk. Mob violence, like the incident in St. Louis, was a constant threat. Randolph was also challenging the Wilson government, whose Justice Department considered him a threat to the administration. Attorney General A. Mitchell Palmer wrote, referring to Randolph, "A certain class of Negro leaders ... constitute themselves a determined and persistent source of radical opposition to the Government and established rule of law and order." Palmer's Justice Department labeled Randolph "the most dangerous Negro in America."

One night in August of 1918, Randolph and Owen spoke at a street rally in Cleveland. They took turns making speeches urging blacks to resist the draft, while followers sold copies of *The Messenger* in the crowd. One of the buyers turned out to be a federal agent. He flipped through the pages of the magazine, finding articles that advocated racial equality. Those were dangerous enough sentiments for the time, but even more shocking to the government man was a report titled "Pro-Germanism Among Negroes." The Justice Department agent broke up the meeting and hauled Randolph from the platform in the middle of his speech.

Randolph and Owen were jailed under the Espionage Act, ostensibly created to prevent spying but used against anyone who spoke out against the war or challenged the status quo. They could have been imprisoned for ten years, but for once, prejudice against African Americans ironically worked to set them free.

The judge they were brought before could not believe two young black men could have composed such eloquent writing, subversive though it was. Randolph and Owen were both twenty-nine at the time, but looked much younger. The judge was sure they had been the unwitting tools of white socialists, who were using the two as a front. He went so far as to order their lawyer to return them home to their parents. Handed their freedom, the two firebrands almost got themselves jailed anyway. When the judge asked them if they could have possibly written the articles in *The Messenger*, they earnestly declared that they had. When he questioned them on their views, they so persuasively made the case for socialism that the judge almost changed his mind and locked them up.

The Department of Justice was not so easily fooled. It called the magazine "by long odds the most able and the most dangerous of all the Negro publications" and kept an ever-growing file on Randolph and Owen.

Black soldiers returning home from the war might have questioned whether the fiery radical ideas of *The*

Messenger were any more dangerous than the status quo in America. When the war ended in 1918 with victory for the United States and its allies, more than 400,000 black soldiers came home. Most of them did not consider themselves radicals, but patriots. They had bet their lives that most Americans would see them that way, too. Instead, they were greeted with the Red Summer of 1919. Racist leaders inflamed fears that returning black soldiers would demand equality and compete for jobs long held by white people. More than twenty race riots broke out that summer, leaving hundreds of people dead. Soldiers who had placed their faith in traditional democracy began to look elsewhere.

Black Americans' growing disillusionment was reflected by the popularity of a radical black leader from Jamaica named Marcus Garvey, who advocated a movement based on returning African Americans to Africa, where they could set up a new nation that had no roots in slavery.

W. E. B. Du Bois wrote that Garvey was a "little fat black man, ugly, but with intelligent eyes and a big head." Garvey's admirers did not find him ugly, nor were they concerned about his girth. They found his ideas compelling, and his speeches on Harlem's street corners mesmerizing.

Garvey was born on August 17, 1887, in the small Jamaican town of St. Ann's Bay. He got an adequate education in public schools, and further enlarged his knowledge with his voracious appetite for reading. At

Marcus Mosiah Garvey was an ostentatious personality whose controversial approach to the growing movement in Harlem was a challenge to Randolph and his followers. *(Library of Congress)*

the age of fourteen, he became a printer's apprentice to his godfather in Kingston. He advanced to the rank of foreman, but when a labor strike broke out in 1909, he joined the strikers. It was the first indication of his lifelong tendency to question and fight established authority. He lived in London for two years, from 1912 to 1914, where he took university classes and met other blacks who criticized discrimination against black people in Western societies. In July of 1914, he traveled back to Jamaica and set up the Universal Negro Improvement Association and African Communities and Imperial League. (The name was later shortened to the Universal Negro Improvement Association, or UNIA.) He wrote to

Booker T. Washington, who invited Garvey to come to America for a speaking tour.

It was Randolph who introduced Garvey to the Harlem street corner speaking circuit, a decision he may later have regretted. One day in 1916, Randolph was speaking to a crowd at the corner of 135th Street and Lenox Avenue when someone pulled at his coat sleeve.

"There's a young man here from Jamaica who wants to be presented to this group," the man said.

"What does he want to talk about?" Randolph asked.

The reply was: "He wants to talk about a movement to develop a back-to-Africa sentiment in America." Always open to young radical street orators, Randolph agreed. The crowd groaned when Randolph announced the new speaker's choice of subject matter, apparently unenthusiastic about the idea of traveling "home" to a continent most had never seen. But Randolph quieted them. "Well, it is good for us to get his position on this question, because we don't know a lot about Africa ourselves," he said.

Garvey took the stage and delivered his speech, his magnificent, booming voice filling the streets. No one had ever heard ideas like Garvey's and not everyone agreed with them. But Asa knew a leader when he saw one. "I could tell from watching him even then that he was one of the greatest propagandists of his time," he later said.

For a brief time, the two became allies. Garvey's UNIA selected Randolph as its delegate to a conference in France, a proposal the State Department vetoed when it refused to issue him a passport. But differences between Garvey's ideas and Randolph's became more apparent as Garvey's movement, and ego, grew.

Garvey dressed flamboyantly and often acted in a way some considered pompous. He sometimes wore green and purple robes, accepting praise from his followers as the "Provisional President" of Africa. At other times, he appeared in paramilitary uniforms and feathered hats as he rode in a chauffeured car through the streets of Harlem. In the end, it was not Garvey's ego as

Garvey's charismatic leadership gave the back-to-Africa movement much of its vitality. Here, a Garvey supporter stands outside UNIA headquarters in New York City. *(Library of Congress)*

much as it was his ideas that began to rankle Randolph and Owen.

The editors of *The Messenger* considered Garvey's call for separation of the races a counterproductive diversion from the struggle for social and economic equality. They also considered his plan to be impractical: how many blacks could really afford to move back to Africa?

Garvey himself dealt the most damaging blow to his reputation in the summer of 1922, when he traveled to Atlanta, Georgia, for a secret meeting with Edward Young Clarke, Imperial Wizard of the Ku Klux Klan. The viciously racist Klan and Garvey's movement had one thing in common—both wanted to separate the races. When he returned to New York, Garvey told the New York *Times* that it was futile for African Americans to resist the Klan's goal of keeping America a country for whites only, and praised the Klansmen for being so forthright. These shocking words marked the beginning of the end for Garvey's movement in the United States.

The Messenger mounted a "Garvey Must Go" campaign. Its pages refuted any past connection with the grandiose segregationist. The editors wrote that African Americans must join together to reject leaders such as Marcus Garvey who ally themselves with racist groups such as the Ku Klux Klan.

Soon after that editorial was published, a mysterious package arrived at the offices of *The Messenger*. Randolph opened it to find a shriveled human hand, a

After World War I, the Ku Klux Klan fused racial hatred to their doctrine of nativism and religious fundamentalism. Although the Klan claimed it was nonpolitical, the group controlled politics in many areas around the country, and in the 1920s elected quite a few state officials and congressmen. At its peak in the mid-1920s, Klan membership was estimated at around four million. This photograph shows Klan members in Washington, D.C., during a planned march in 1922.

message warning him that he was being watched and hinting that he could be lynched or have his own hand cut off. The Ku Klux Klan signed it, but Randolph suspected that Garvey or his followers were really behind the threats. Unruffled by the bizarre package, he continued to attack Garvey over the next several years, even after Garvey's movement began to sputter. In 1927, the government sealed Garvey's doom when it indicted him for mail fraud. He was deported and his UNIA collapsed.

Randolph and Owen had outlasted their rival, but the effort took valuable time away from their effort to achieve racial equality. Newspaper accounts that might have been devoted to the struggle had instead reported on the rift between the leaders. During the magazine's battles with Garvey, other African-American publications were founded, with content that challenged *The Messenger*'s assertion that it was the "only" radical magazine for African Americans. Its influence began to wane.

The years 1923 and 1924 brought sad times for Randolph, both professionally and personally. Chandler Owen left New York for Chicago, where he became a newspaper writer. His absence left a vacuum at the magazine. The next year, Randolph's father died. Asa was now a national leader, but he wondered about the direction his future efforts should take. The answer would come in 1925, when America's most respected black workers brought Randolph his next battle.

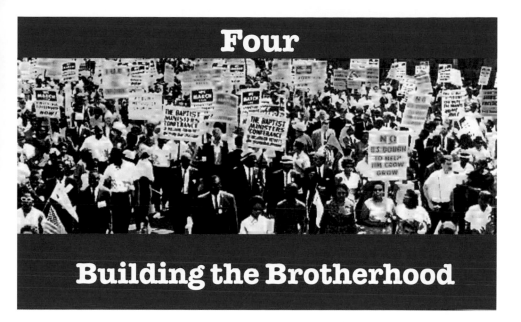

Four

Building the Brotherhood

One morning in June of 1925, a tall, broad-shouldered man in a white Panama hat stopped Asa Randolph on his way to *The Messenger* office. He introduced himself as Ashley Totten, a porter for the Pullman Company, which ran a line of luxury railroad sleeping cars.

Totten told Asa that he was an admirer and longtime reader of his magazine, and that he had a favor to ask. Would Randolph be willing to speak to a meeting of the Pullman Porters Athletic Association? Totten wanted the radical editor to address the porters about ways to organize and bargain with management. Randolph agreed without hesitation. He never passed up a chance to help organize the black working class.

Most people in the street would have been surprised to overhear such a conversation. How could the Pullman porters be dissatisfied with their lot? They were widely considered the best-employed black workers in the country. They traveled all over the country, and earned steady wages in tips; most owned their own homes and ranked among the most highly respected members of their communities. But in reality, the public perception of the porters was a combination of ignorance about their working conditions and low expectations for African Americans.

The founder of the company, George Mortimer Pullman, had indeed given freed slaves their first jobs. In 1858, he had come up with the idea of creating luxury sleeping cars to replace the rough sleeping conditions of passenger trains. The Pullman sleeping car had decorated ceilings, chandeliers, and carpeted floors, and initially seemed a little too fancy for most passengers. Then, in the midst of a national tragedy, a quirk of fate changed Pullman's fortunes. When President Abraham Lincoln was assassinated in 1865, state officials in Illinois—the place of Lincoln's birth—wanted to transport his body for burial in the most magnificent railroad car available. The best available at the time was the Pioneer model of Pullman's car, and the attention it drew during the long journey from Washington to Springfield was a publicity coup for the company.

Affluent passengers wanted the most in luxury, including personal service. In 1867, Pullman hit on the idea of hiring ex-slaves as porters. He reasoned that they would be naturally used to lives of service, and happy

Pullman Company founder George M. Pullman. *(Courtesy of Getty Images.)*

at the chance for jobs. By 1920, the Pullman Company was the largest employer of black workers in the United States. But the heritage of slavery made the porters and maids as vulnerable to exploitation as other workers. Pullman took advantage of their weak bargaining position to keep them working long hours for low wages.

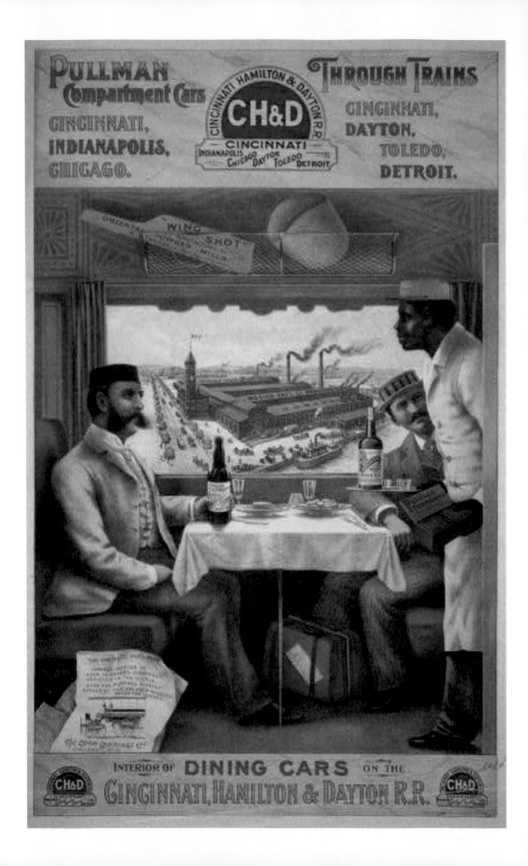

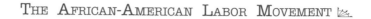

In this photograph, Pullman porter Alfred McMillian readies an upper berth on the Capital Limited train to Chicago. *(Library of Congress)*

Porters' wages in 1919 were sixty dollars a month, with the possibility of making more in tips. Even with tips added, however, they made no more than two-thirds of the amount generally accepted as the minimum necessary to maintain a respectable standard of living for

Opposite: This advertisement showcases the luxurious Pullman car as well as the famed service of the Pullman porter. *(Library of Congress)*

white workers. They had to work four hundred hours a month before being considered for overtime. For a train scheduled to leave at midnight, they had to arrive early in the evening to help prepare for departure—but they did not begin to get paid until the train actually departed. A porter often did not get paid for the five hours of labor he did prior to the start of his shift; most rarely got a glimpse of their families.

The Pullman Company executives knew they were getting a bargain from their porters and maids and did all they could to polish their public image. The hope was that the prestige earned by being a Pullman porter would compensate for the low wages. They referred to their employees as the Pullman "family" and even organized a Plan of Employee Representation that, in reality, was really a means of warding off a real union.

A union with genuine power was just what Ashley Totten and other disgruntled porters were seeking. When Randolph spoke to the Pullman Porters Athletic Association, he got a lively round of applause. Afterward, several of them asked him to lead them in their fight for a union. He politely declined; at that point his life revolved around *The Messenger*. He also thought the leader of the union should come from within the ranks of porters. "I am not sure that I had ever seen a Pullman car then—much less ridden in one," he later recalled.

The porters had managed to pique Randolph's interest. In the July and August 1925 issues of *The Messenger*, he published two articles about their plight: "The

Case of the Pullman Porter" and "Pullman Porters Need Their Own Union." Porters read the articles with joy, and discussed the possibility of Randolph becoming their leader. Ashley Totten approached Randolph again about organizing a union, and this time, he accepted.

On August 25, 1925, Randolph led a meeting at the Imperial Lodge of Elks on West 129th Street where the Brotherhood of Sleeping Car Porters was formed. A crowd of five hundred showed up for the inaugural meeting—but not all were there to launch a union. The Pullman Company had sent spies to report back on what was said. Randolph, who suspected informers would be present, made sure no porter spoke.

"I told the men I didn't want one porter to open his mouth in the meeting, lest the stool pigeons reported them to the Pullman Company," he said later. "So I ran the whole meeting myself." He did everything from giving the invocation to introducing guest speakers and delivering the main speech. He announced the new union's demands, including a minimum pay of $150 monthly and an end to unpaid hours. "At the end of the meeting, I moved the vote of thanks, said the benediction, and told everyone to go home and not hold any discussions on the street corners."

The following day, two hundred porters came to the offices of *The Messenger*, now serving as the union's headquarters, to join up. Their dues made up the beginnings of the organization's treasury and Randolph did additional fund-raising. The Garland Fund, a liberal

Brotherhood member and organizer Milton P. Webster. *(Library of Congress)*

organization, donated $10,000. Randolph used some of the money to launch a speaking tour to the cities where Pullman trains stopped.

Ashley Totten told Randolph which were the most important porters to meet in each city. Particularly important was Milton Price Webster of Chicago, a tall, powerfully built man who looked more like a boxer than the shrewd political insider he was. Webster was the leader of the Republicans in the city's Sixth Ward and

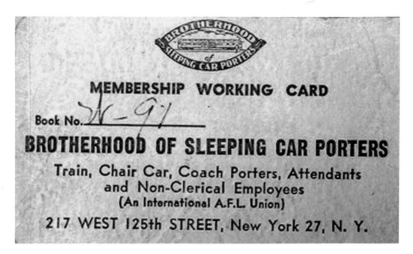

A union card belonging to a member of the Brotherhood. *(A. Philip Randolph Institute)*

claimed to know "all the crooks and all the different angles" around the city. At first he was skeptical about Randolph's leadership, but the first time Webster heard him speak to a crowd he was won over. Webster organized a Chicago branch of the Brotherhood that was second in size only to the main office in New York.

At first, the Pullman Company did not think it had to do anything but ignore the Brotherhood. As Randolph and his followers demonstrated their determination, company executives mounted a campaign of threats against union organizers and smears against Randolph's reputation. Anyone reported attending a meeting or caught with a union card ran the risk of being fired. Even being seen with a union member could cost a porter his job.

Pullman management (George Pullman was long dead) sent out letters attacking Randolph's character. They found his past writing fertile ground for the smear campaign, since he had taken many controversial positions. The company charged that he was a dangerous radical using the porters for his own ends. They called him a Communist, an atheist, and a traitor to the war effort in World War I. Randolph pressed on despite the personal attacks, telling union members that from the moment he offered to lead the organization he "knew that slanderers would attempt to blacken my character with infamy."

Attacks from other African-American journalists stung Randolph worse. In the beginning, the black press almost unanimously condemned the Brotherhood. Pullman began to pour advertising dollars into black newspapers, and readers often saw anti-Brotherhood editorials in the same issues with full-page ads for the company. The influence of *The Messenger* helped Randolph to gradually turn the tide. He used his pages to ridicule the dominant Chicago African-American newspaper, *Chicago Defender,* as the Chicago "Surrender." He pointed out the Pullman Company's tactic of buying favor from supporting newspapers, and revealed that another black newspaper, the *Chicago Whip,* was owned by Pullman lawyers. Slowly, as the movement progressed, many of the black-owned papers switched sides.

Randolph toned down his message and stopped mentioning socialism in order to appeal to moderate supporters of labor. "This movement is not radical, except in the sense that the whole trade union movement is fundamentally radical," he said. "The porters also want a voice in the determination of the conditions under which they work, the abolition of the Pullman feudalistic paternalism, a relic of the old master-slave relationship."

Randolph's leadership brought results. Within two years of the meeting at the Elks lodge, membership soared to seven thousand. Most of the porters outside of the South were members. Randolph then attempted to use the Brotherhood's numbers to force Pullman to deal. He turned to a new law that had been passed to prevent disruption of the nation's rail service. The Railway Labor Act of 1926 provided for a mediation board to settle disputes between labor and management. To establish grounds for a settlement hearing, Randolph had to show he represented the workers. He first wrote the Pullman Company to ask for a meeting. Predictably, the company did not respond. He then appealed to the mediation board. The board ruled Randolph's request legitimate, and appointed Edward Morrow, a former Kentucky governor, to head the investigation.

Morrow opened the hearings in December of 1926. The Pullman Company insisted its employees already had an organization, the Plan of Employee Representation. It claimed that there was no dispute between Pullman and the porters. After all, the company pointed out, eighty-five percent of its workers had voted for the plan. But the management-controlled employee plan was a far cry from a union. Randolph produced nine hundred affidavits from company workers who said that the company had forced them to vote for the plan.

Randolph in conversation with Edward Morrow during the investigation of the Pullman labor dispute. *(Library of Congress)*

Morrow adjourned the hearing to study the evidence. When he asked the sides to reconvene in 1927, the Pullman Company refused to attend. A loophole in the law worked to the employer's benefit—Morrow had no legal authority to force the company to attend, unless an emergency threatened a railway stoppage. Pullman thought it had found a way to end the mediation. Randolph had no choice but to call their bluff and use the most potent weapon he had—the threat of a strike.

Striking a company as powerful as Pullman could be dangerous. A generation before, in 1894, a strike against the company had left several dead, and had been crushed by a combination of federal troops and Pullman-paid enforcers. Randolph knew he would have to make a strong case to convince the workers to risk their jobs and possibly their lives. By this time, however, his stature had increased with the porters, and most trusted his skill, admired his eloquence and affectionately dubbed him "Chief." He won the membership over to the idea of a strike, and announced it in May of 1928.

The threat of a strike was enough to compel Pullman back into talks with the Brotherhood. But the company's representatives offered the union no concessions—no wage increases or increased overtime pay. They suspected that Randolph could not actually carry out a strike. The mediation board refused to declare a state of emergency.

Randolph realized the long odds he would face striking against a company armed with deep coffers. There were plenty of scabs willing to take union jobs from workers who walked out. Reluctantly, he called off the strike. In July, the board dropped the case.

It had been a rough year for Randolph. His brother James had contracted diphtheria and died in January. Nothing else that happened that year matched his sorrow at losing his beloved childhood companion and mentor. Even so, he knew he had let down the Brotherhood. When the government board dropped the porters' case, Asa said, it was "next to the saddest moment of his life."

Five

Porter versus Pullman

Randolph and the Brotherhood had suffered a terrible setback. He put on a brave face on the defeat, defiantly declaring "nothing can keep us from winning." In reality, he had to struggle just to keep the Brotherhood of Sleeping Car Porters alive.

In the months after Randolph had called off the strike membership in the union dropped from seven thousand to less than twenty-five hundred. *The Messenger,* which had become the unofficial mouthpiece of the Brotherhood, lost the readers who thought its editor had become too obsessed with the union. Even many of the porters stopped reading it after the strike fell through. Short of money to pay rent and printing costs, the magazine closed in 1928. For the first time in years, Randolph had lost his access to the printed word. His published opinions remained on hold until the following year, when the Brotherhood founded the *Black Worker*, which called itself "The Mouthpiece of the Negro Workers of America."

Those who remained loyal to the union paid a high price. Vengeful in victory, the Pullman Company sought out porters who had voted for the union and fired them.

The national organizers fared little better. Randolph's controversial reputation cost Lucille Randolph's beauty shop more and more customers, until finally she was forced to close. Milton Webster's Chicago office supplied the New York office with funds from its own sparse coffers. Often Randolph could not even afford carfare downtown to research his articles in the public library. The suits he wore on his speaking tours became threadbare. His shabby appearance saddened longtime followers. When the Brotherhood failed to make payments on its offices, Randolph and his staff were evicted, and their furniture and records tossed out on the sidewalk. From there, the office moved to a small apartment, where it subsisted on the profits from Saturday "rent sales" of such food as chitterlings, stew, and potato salad.

Union organizers faced violence as well as poverty and hunger. In April of 1929, two men ambushed Ashley Totten on the street in Kansas City, smashing him in the face with billy clubs. The muscular Totten almost wrestled one of the clubs away from his attackers, but lost his grip and fell to the ground, where slashing blows broke his jaw and knocked out several teeth. After that, Randolph transferred Totten to a desk job at the New York office.

Totten wore the scars of the assault for the rest of his life.

Randolph could have gotten funds from white organizations friendly to his cause, such as the Garland Fund, which originally gave a grant to the Brotherhood. But Randolph had revised his views about accepting money from outsiders. Black unionists must "pay the price and bear the brunt of their own struggle," he insisted. This stubborn insistence on the purity of their struggle frustrated some of his supporters.

Randolph realized the Brotherhood could not succeed without allies. In 1929, he approached the American Federation of Labor (AFL) to ask that the black union be admitted. Longtime readers of *The Messenger* recalled that he had once criticized the AFL as an organization that

AFL president, William Green. *(Library of Congress)*

encouraged segregation in the workforce. He had even sarcastically referred to it as the "American Separation of Labor." Even so, AFL President William Green agreed with the porters' cause and used his influence to get the Brotherhood accepted.

In the fall of 1929, a national economic catastrophe struck. During America's boom years of the 1920s, many people had made fortunes speculating on the stock market. Brokers had encouraged such financial gambling by giving investors loans for payment of a small percentage of a stock's worth, a practice called margin trading. Investors could spend their life savings on such risky ventures if they liked. Euphoric speculators seemed to forget that if stocks could skyrocket so rapidly, they could plummet just as quickly.

Rumors of a downturn spread through the market in October, triggering a wave of desperate selling. Prices dropped so rapidly that investors large and small were ruined. On October 29, the New York Stock Exchange suffered its greatest losses in history. By the end of the day, stock values had declined by billions.

The resulting Great Depression, in which millions of jobs disappeared and thousands of banks had to close, might have seemed like a death knell to the Brotherhood. Even workers who managed to stay employed felt their economic security threatened by the Depression. In some ways, though, the economic collapse benefited the Pullman Porters and the union movement in general. It was hard to get the status quo changed when most people were benefiting from the economy. But with so many people suffering financially, the nation was suddenly looking for a change. Republican President Herbert Hoover was blamed for the Depression, and in the election year of 1932, Franklin Delano Roosevelt of New

In his efforts to help the country recover from the Great Depression, President Franklin D. Roosevelt worked to spur economic growth through government-aided projects.

York offered to give Americans a "New Deal." To lift the nation out of the Depression, the New Deal government would take a greater role in social and economic affairs, sponsoring public construction projects to give people jobs. From Randolph's perspective, it did not hurt that Roosevelt strongly courted the union during his campaign. When he won a landslide victory, Roosevelt entered office owing a debt to his union supporters.

Roosevelt and the Democratic Party did not disappoint. In June of 1933, Congress passed two laws that strengthened the hand of organized railroad workers: the Emergency Railroad Transportation Act (ERTA) and the National Industrial Recovery Act (NIRA). NIRA guaranteed railroad workers the right to elect representatives, form unions, and bargain with management.

A loophole in NIRA almost let the Pullman Company off the hook. Because its product was a luxury car,

Pullman's lobbyists succeeded in getting it classified as a hotel service instead of a railway company. Randolph refused to let this piece of trickery slip through. He wrote letters of protest to Congress and the president. His alliance with the AFL paid off; its president, William Green, used his power to lobby on the Brotherhood's behalf. In 1934, the act was amended and Pullman was classified as a railway company.

Once again, Randolph wrote Pullman management and asked for a meeting. The company tried its 1920s tactics again, simply refusing the request. "There is no occasion for a conference with you," a Pullman spokesman wrote back.

But one-sided rejections no longer worked under the new law. Randolph again appealed to the mediation board in Washington, which this time ordered an immediate election to determine which group had the right to represent the porters. On June 27, 1935, the porters voted by secret ballot. Nearly six thousand porters voted for the Brotherhood of Sleeping Car Porters, against a mere fourteen hundred for the Pullman's employee association.

Randolph had pulled out a victory that had looked impossible just a few years before. The press trumpeted his success story, making him the most heralded black leader in America.

But the Pullman management had not agreed to honor any of the Brotherhood's demands, only to obey the law. They made negotiations with the union representatives as tough as possible, digging in their heels about every point. They clearly had a low opinion of their opposition. The law might demand Pullman executives sit down at the table, but that did not mean the porters would get anything significant in return.

On the morning of July 29, 1935, Randolph and his officers walked into a conference room of the Pullman Company on Adams Street in Chicago. Pullman wanted to make the porters feel out of their league in this meeting with high-paid executives and company lawyers, and at first, they succeeded. One of the porters later confessed, "We had no experience with high finance, we didn't know what a million dollars was like."

Brotherhood member C. L. Dellums. *(Library of Congress)*

C. L. Dellums, who headed the Oakland division of the Brotherhood, also felt at a disadvantage—though he had confidence in Randolph's leadership: "Here was this handful of guys around Randolph. None of us was prepared, none had any special training, none really educated. But here we were around this wonderful man."

Randolph certainly carried his weight in the talks, but he faced some disadvantages too. Pullman President E. G. Carry was an aggressive and often combative bargainer, given to putting his shoes up on the table and letting fly with a string of curse words. Randolph did not even like to be caught slumping, certainly not during an official discussion, and he rarely used vulgar language. At first, he did not know how to respond to Carry's aggressive and crude baiting. Randolph and his tougher lieutenants soon worked out a strategy. When talks were going smoothly, Randolph held the floor. But when Carry or any of the others began blasting him with foul or abusive language, he would turn to Dellums or Milton Webster to play the bulldog.

One day the meeting turned into a fierce shouting match, with Carry shaking his finger across the table and cursing Randolph, while Randolph shook his fist at Carry. Randolph knew he could never win an argument in this style. He gave the floor to Dellums.

"He said 'C. L., did you want to make an observation?'" Dellums recalled later. "But I knew what he meant. He meant that this baby [Carry] needs some cursing right now, and the Chief couldn't do it. And he knew that was right down my alley. Well, I gave it to that Carry. I gave it to him so good that two minutes later the mediator broke up the meeting."

The company spent two years stalling the Brotherhood. It thought it could triumph by waiting out the porters until they lost faith in their leadership again. Pullman also pinned its hopes on the courts, which were then determining if the new railway law was constitutional. Executives would postpone meetings, trigger walkouts, and attempt to drown the porters in paperwork. They would break their proposals up into separate documents, so the Brotherhood representatives ended up walking out of meetings with hundreds of sheets of paper, some containing only two or three lines.

In March of 1937, the Supreme Court ruled the Railway Labor Act constitutional. The Pullman executives realized that the clock had run down on their attempts to stall. They at last began in earnest to negotiate. On August 25, they signed a new contract that granted a reduction in the work month from four hundred to two hundred and fifty hours, along with an annual wage package that totaled $1,250,000.

The Brotherhood logo. *(A. Philip Randolph Institute)*

Letters of congratulations poured into Randolph's New York office. People who had known neither Randolph nor his lieutenants turned to look when they passed on the street. When the Brotherhood held rallies now, everybody wanted to get as close as possible. "People we never heard of before wanted to sit on the platform," Milton Webster recalled. "They took us down to the Waldorf Astoria, a hotel that we had been passing by for the last twenty years. Had everything from Coca-Cola to champagne."

The publicity over the Pullman dispute transformed Asa Philip Randolph from a street radical to the most popular black leader in America. When eight hundred representatives of black associations met in Chicago in

Randolph is photographed here (*front center*) with railroad workers and Brotherhood members in Washington, D.C., after his successful negotiations with the Pullman Company. *(Library of Congress)*

February of 1936 to form the National Negro Congress (NNC), they elected Randolph president even though he was not present. Nonetheless, he accepted the position.

The NNC never lived up to its initial promise as a national organization representing African Americans. Some of its members were Communists, following a philosophy that the socialist Randolph had differences with. He further alienated some of its members by giving speeches on the growing threat posed by Adolf Hitler and Nazi Germany, a menace they considered less dangerous than American racism. When, in 1940, the NNC became largely dominated by Communists, Randolph resigned the presidency. Communists were suspect in American and Randolph felt black people had enough to overcome without the stigma of being Communist, too.

Randolph still believed the union was the most important frontier in the fight for racial equality. Now that the Brotherhood had achieved full recognition as the porters' union, it would have to prove itself as an equal among unions. Even as Randolph had been working his way toward a contract with the Pullman Company, he had also waded into conflicts with the American Federation of Labor.

Criticizing the AFL in the 1930s seemed to be an ungrateful act to many union leaders. AFL President William Green was putting his prestige on the line to pressure Congress on the railroad bills. But the fact was that most unions still discriminated. In fact, the Depression hit blacks harder than white workers because so many unions denied them protection. One out of every ten white workers had a union card, compared to one in fifty blacks. Thirty AFL unions would not allow African Americans to join. Unions like the Brotherhood of Locomotive Firemen and Engineers went a step farther, making management sign contracts forbidding the hiring of black workers.

Randolph wanted the unions to hire organizers to create black unions in the South, an undertaking that would have been physically dangerous. He wanted unions that excluded blacks thrown out of the AFL. The color barrier was "unsound, defenseless, undemocratic, illegal and un-American," he thundered at one convention.

He persuaded Green to appoint a committee to study union discrimination. The committee came back in almost full agreement with Randolph. It called for a three-part plan to abolish union prejudice against African Americans: unions that discriminated would have to change their rules, the AFL would bar unions that refused blacks, and the AFL would set up a committee that would educate workers about the importance of racial unity. But Green turned the report over to another union official who rewrote it so completely that the next draft called only for education. Randolph was furious, and dragged the next convention into the late hours of the morning fighting to keep the watered-down report from being left in the "unfinished business" pile.

"The American Federation of Labor will not be able to hold its head up and face the world," he argued, "so long as it permits any sections of workers in America to be discriminated against because they happen to be black." But his words had little effect—by this time of night, members were annoyed, sleepy, and ready to go home. This was not the only time Randolph would inconvenience representatives of a labor conference. He had a knack for setting off heated, angry sessions that stretched into the night.

John L. Lewis of the United Mine Workers and David Dubinsky of the International Ladies Garment Workers Union headed unions that were integrated. They too believed the AFL should stand up for racial equality in membership. On race and many other issues, they picked as many fights with the AFL as Randolph did. But when John L. Lewis led a rebellion against the AFL and founded the Congress of Industrial Organization (CIO), Randolph declined his invitation to join. Because the AFL was the more prejudiced of the two union organizations, the AFL was where he felt he should make his stand.

Randolph was again left mostly alone in the long struggle to fully integrate the AFL unions. This fight would stretch over decades, much longer than the one for recognition of the Brotherhood of Sleeping Car Porters. Meanwhile, the world outside the union halls was changing. While Randolph fought the AFL for racial equality, national leaders saw another world war on the horizon.

Six

The President's Order

America found itself in a curious position on the issue of race as the 1940s began. While segregationist politicians fought to keep racist institutions intact in the United States, the greatest international threat came from one of history's most murderous racists.

Since Adolf Hitler's rise to power in Germany in the early 1930s, the dictator had preached the superiority of the "Nordic," or Northern European, people. He despised Jewish people, and would soon fill his concentration camps with them. In 1939, his armies invaded Poland and began an attempt to conquer Europe and Great Britain. Meanwhile, Imperial Japan allied with Germany and mounted similar attacks against China and other parts of the Far East. President Roosevelt and others realized America would soon have to defend its allies, and defense factories began cranking out planes, rifles, and bullets at top speed.

The military buildup helped the nation reach a level of robust employment that finally ended the Great Depression. It was robust and good economic times— for everyone but African Americans. Defense plants employed no skilled black workers; those few who did get jobs worked mostly as janitors.

"We have not had a Negro worker in twenty-five years and do not plan to start now," said a steel company executive, expressing a common feeling at the time.

The government announced that defense plants would need 250,000 workers, but they still refused to hire blacks. Over 500,000 black Americans who might have been employed in the defense industry remained idle in 1942, according to a Federal Security Agency publication. Some African Americans made their displeasure known with protests outside factories. One sign of the times was a placard reading:

HITLER MUST OWN THIS PLANT,
NEGROES CAN'T WORK HERE
IF WE MUST FIGHT, WHY CAN'T WE WORK?

Most unions gave black workers no more help than management did. When black people marched outside the Boeing Aircraft plant in Seattle, demanding jobs, the district organizer of the International Association of Machinists declared, "Labor has been asked to make many sacrifices in this war, and made them gladly, but this sacrifice . . . is too great."

Even with Hitler's promise to topple Western democracy, some bigots considered the threat to white supremacy more dangerous. The mayor of Shreveport, Louisiana, rejected a federal grant because it would have required construction companies to consider black applicants. "Of equal importance to winning the war is the necessity of keeping Negroes out of skilled jobs," he said.

While defense companies tried to prepare for war using all-white workforces, the armed forces continued to keep black soldiers behind the color barrier. A nationwide draft went into effect in September of 1940, but African Americans entered under the same conditions as World War I. They fought in segregated units, under white commanders. Black soldiers who drilled in the South faced jeers from civilians.

Aviation cadets and Tuskegee Army Air Field enlisted personnel study a P-40 engine in a class about liquid-cooled motors. *(Library of Congress)*

Randolph and other black leaders bristled at how little had changed in the more than twenty years since black soldiers had trooped off to World War I, with the false expectation that their sacrifice would earn them full citizenship. The same month the draft went into effect, the Brotherhood of Sleeping Car Porters passed a resolution at their fifteenth annual convention at the Harlem YMCA. It called for the president, Congress, and heads of government agencies to ban racial discrimination in the Army, Navy, and Air Corps. One of the people who attended the Brotherhood meeting was First Lady Eleanor Roosevelt.

Mrs. Roosevelt helped her husband's administration reach out to minorities. She was highly sensitive to the needs of the underprivileged. The president gained a reputation as being a liberal administrator, with compassion for the poor and working class, but it was Eleanor who mingled more with the people, becoming one of the most admired American women of her time. She made a speech at the Brotherhood convention, promising cooperation. She reported the event to her husband and his secretary, who promptly set up a meeting at the White House that included both military leaders and black leaders. Roosevelt invited Randolph as well as Walter White of the NAACP and T. Arnold Hill of the National Urban League.

The meeting took place on September 27. Despite Eleanor Roosevelt's high expectations, Randolph, White, and Hill left feeling disappointed. Roosevelt had promised little. Even worse, Roosevelt's secretary Stephen Early later called a press conference that insulted the reputations of the black leaders. He told reporters, "the policy of the War Department is not to intermingle colored and white enlisted personnel in the same regimental organization." He then added, "the segregation policy was approved after Roosevelt conferred with Walter White [and] two other Negroes."

The statement astonished the African-American public. How could their leaders have endorsed a policy of military segregation? This duplicity on the part of the Roosevelt Administration damaged Randolph, White, and Hill's ability to lead. They demanded a public clarification from the White House but none was forthcoming. They then demanded that Early be fired for misrepresenting them, but Roosevelt refused that as well. The president finally sent a letter saying that Early's statement had been misinterpreted. Roosevelt said blacks would be trained for highly skilled jobs, such as aviation, and they would also be given the chance to be promoted to the officer ranks.

This had little to do with the point of the original meeting, at least as the three black leaders saw it. But they realized they had no leverage against the White House now. Randolph dutifully sent a letter of thanks, and the three read the letter about "misinterpretation" into their public speeches in order to salvage their reputations.

The sting lingered in December of 1940, as Randolph

and Milton Webster rode a train from Washington to tour Brotherhood divisions in the South. Webster was looking out the window of the train in a solemn mood, remembering how white bigots had run his family out of the South when he was a boy. It was Randolph who broke the silence.

"You know, Web," he said, "calling on the President and holding those conferences are not going to get us anywhere." Webster agreed, and Randolph continued. "We are going to have to do something about it," he said. Webster did not reply, but knew Randolph was hatching a plan. "I think we ought to get 10,000 Negroes to march on Washington in protest, march down Pennsylvania Avenue," Randolph continued. "What do you think of that?"

Webster thought it was a fine idea, but asked, "Where are you going to get 10,000 Negroes?"

"I think we can get them," Randolph said, and that ended the conversation for the time.

But Randolph brought it up again, in one of the riskier cities to talk about black marches—Savannah, Georgia. The Brotherhood's leaders called a public meeting announcing plans for the march. By this time, their demands had expanded beyond desegregation of the military to equal opportunity for jobs in the defense industry. Black newspapers ran stories and editorials on the march, and the idea was picking up national momentum by the time the two returned to New York.

From January through early spring of 1941, Randolph

issued press releases about the march to newspapers across the country. He wrote:

> In this period of power politics, nothing counts but pressure, more pressure, and still more pressure, through the tactic and strategy of broad, organized, aggressive mass action behind the vital and important issues of the Negro. To this end we propose that ten thousand Negroes MARCH ON WASHINGTON FOR JOBS IN NATIONAL DEFENSE AND EQUAL INTEGRATION IN THE FIGHTING FORCES OF THE UNITED STATES.
>
> An "all-out" thundering march on Washington, ending in a monster and huge demonstration at Lincoln's Memorial will shake up white America. It will shake up official Washington . . . It will gain respect for the Negro people . . . It will create a new sense of self-respect among Negroes.

Randolph's press release underscored the importance of the equality in the military to the economic well-being of black Americans:

> The Negroes stake in national defense is big. It consists of jobs, thousands of jobs. It may represent millions, yes, hundreds of millions of dollars in wages. It consists of new industrial opportunities and hope. This is worth fighting for. Most important and vital to all, Negroes, by the mobilization and coordination of their mass power, can cause PRESIDENT ROOSEVELT TO ISSUE AN EXECUTIVE ORDER ABOLISHING DISCRIMINATION IN

ALL GOVERNMENT DEPARTMENTS, ARMY, NAVY, AIR CORPS, AND NATIONAL DEFENSE JOBS.

He set the date of the march for July 1, 1941. The black press, once so critical of Randolph, almost unanimously hailed his idea. The *Chicago Defender* wrote: "This is the time, the place, the issue and the method."

And ordinary black citizens answered the call. From across the country, they wrote Randolph's Brotherhood headquarters asking for specifics on how to organize

The March on Washington Committee set up fundraising venues around the country, such as this bookshop in Harlem, which also served as Randolph's organizing headquarters. *(Library of Congress)*

and help. Randolph set up the March on Washington Committee (MOWC) to handle the details of the event.

A poster promoting MOWC involvement.

News of the march reached the Roosevelt White House as early as January, but neither the president nor his advisors took it seriously at first. They made no public statements and waited to gauge reaction. Randolph pressed the issue by sending a request that the president's circle must have found bothersome: would President Roosevelt agree to address the marchers at the Lincoln Memorial? The message achieved its effect, and Randolph received word that the administration was worried about the dangers the march might bring. The main threat, of course, was that it would embarrass an administration supposedly dedicated to human rights.

Once again, Eleanor Roosevelt became the administration's emissary to the black leaders. She asked Randolph how the marchers would be fed and housed. He said he assumed they would stay in hotels and eat in restaurants. His only role was to get them to Washington. The First Lady's report could have brought no comfort to the White House. Most of the hotels and diners in Washington were still white-only. Marchers who insisted on integrating such establishments could ignite a race war in the capital.

Randolph was actually taking more care to avoid racial conflict than he let it seem. He asked the Washington branch of the committee to seek out African-American churches and schools to feed and house the marchers. However, he did not want to do any thing to alleviate official Washington's fear of a militant invasion by thousands of angry black Americans.

He began to suspect that the FBI was trailing his movements. Instead of avoiding federal agents, Randolph made himself all the more public, in the hope of creating more jitters in Washington's official circles. He met supporters openly on Lenox, Seventh, and Eighth avenues, went into barbershops and theater lobbies, always stopping to buttonhole people for a few words about the march. And rather than downplay the risks, he upped the ante. By the end of May he was no longer talking about the ten thousand marchers, but one hundred thousand.

Randolph succeeded in alarming Washington. President Roosevelt sent Eleanor, along with a handful of officials, to New York to meet with the march leaders. The official delegation met with Randolph and Walter White of the NAACP at City Hall on June 13, 1941. Mrs. Roosevelt assured Randolph and White that she agreed with their goals, but thought a march could lead to serious trouble. The majority of police in the capital

Randolph walks with Eleanor Roosevelt and New York mayor Fiorello La Guardia during one of Randolph's visits to Washington to meet with the president.

were white southerners, a dangerous addition to any mass racial gathering. Eleanor Roosevelt had counted on her reputation as a champion of civil rights to sway Randolph, but it was not enough this time. Randolph said he could not back down because he had made promises to his followers. He would not call off the march unless the president signed an executive order banning discrimination in the military.

Time was running short. When Eleanor's delegation came back with this message from the march leaders, the president realized he would have to meet them himself. Five days later, a group including Randolph, White, and New York Mayor Fiorello La Guardia walked into the White House for a meeting with President Roosevelt and his war secretaries. Roosevelt was a charming man and he attempted to disarm Randolph. He asked which class Randolph was in at Harvard. (Randolph had never attended Harvard, but a common myth had circulated that he had, perhaps because of his cultured manner of speech.)

Roosevelt then began to regale the group with old political anecdotes. Randolph knew that the president did not have all day for small talk, and, suspecting that delay was part of the president's strategy, cut him short as politely as he knew how.

"Mr. President, time is running on," he said. "You are quite busy, I know. But what we want to talk about is the problem of jobs for Negroes in defense industries. Our people are being turned away at factory gates because they are colored. They can't live with this thing. Now, what are you going to do about it?"

Roosevelt asked Randolph what he wanted him to do. "Mr. President, we want you to do something that will enable Negro workers to get work in these plants." Roosevelt offered to talk to the heads of the factories. Randolph had heard more than enough from factory executives to know this was simply another stalling tactic. He said, "Mr. President, we want you to issue an executive order making it mandatory that Negroes be permitted to work in these plants."

Roosevelt replied that he could not possibly do that: "If I issue an executive order for you, then there'll be no end to other groups coming in here and asking me to issue executive orders for them, too. In any event, I couldn't do anything unless you called off this march of yours. Questions like this can't be settled with a sledge hammer."

"I'm sorry, Mr. President, the march cannot be called off."

"How many people do you plan to bring?" Roosevelt asked.

"One hundred thousand, Mr. President." The president could not believe his ears. He asked White if the figure could possibly be accurate. White assured him it was.

Roosevelt dropped the pretense of jovial discourse and warned Randolph that his plans could get people killed. Not if the president addressed the crowd himself, Randolph argued. Roosevelt curtly refused. Mayor La Guardia weighed in on Randolph's side, saying that it was clear the march would go on unless the president signed the executive order.

Roosevelt finally relented. He had the group dismissed to an anteroom to work out satisfactory wording for an order. The work was too complex to be achieved in a single sitting, so a young government lawyer named Joseph L. Rauh Jr. was appointed as Roosevelt's emissary to work with the black leaders on succeeding drafts. Randolph was not easy to please; he turned down one version after another as Rauh read them from Washington over the telephone.

Rauh finally produced a draft that Randolph considered satisfactory. On June 25, the president issued Executive Order 8802, which stated in part: "there shall be no discrimination in the employment of workers in defense industries or government because of race, creed, color or national origin." It placed the burden of compliance on employers and unions. On July 19, the president appointed the Fair Employment Practices Committee to enforce the new rules.

Keeping his word, Randolph cancelled the march. The decision came as a great disappointment to some of the younger members of his movement, who thought the older man had sold out. These included Bayard Rustin, an opinionated and fiery young disciple who would later become Randolph's top lieutenant. But at age fifty-one, Randolph knew better than his younger comrades did how important it was to keep the pact with the first president who had negotiated with African-American leaders.

It had not been an easy process. "Who is this guy Randolph?" attorney Rauh had exploded in frustration at one point, when Asa had turned down yet another draft of the order. "What the hell has he got over the President of the United States?" What Randolph had, of course, was the confidence of millions of African Americans, a bond that grew stronger as he continued to get results.

Seven

The Double V

Randolph's success in forcing President Roosevelt to lift racial discrimination in the military industry helped to light a guiding torch for the African-American struggle toward equality. It was one thing for black leaders to be invited to sit down with the president and take a few minutes of his time, and for him to spend a while sympathizing with their grievances. It was quite another for any such leader to force a president to back up his words with a change in policy.

In the summer of 1941, praise showered down on Randolph from newspapers throughout the United States. The *Amsterdam News,* from New York City, wrote, "A. Philip Randolph, courageous champion of the rights of his people, takes the helm as the nation's No. 1 Negro leader." W. E. B. Du Bois, who had traded barbs with

Randolph, whose success with Roosevelt made him an elder statesman in the labor movement, meets with other labor organizers. *From left to right:* Ashley Totten, an unidentified man, Randolph, and Maida Springer-Kemp, a union official for International Packing House workers. *(Library of Congress)*

Randolph during his days with *The Messenger,* said the actions which compelled Roosevelt's order 8802, were "the most astonishing in our later leadership." Another writer pointed out that the Brotherhood had become "a kind of cathedral" for the Negro rights movement.

As the acclaim poured into the Brotherhood's New York offices, Randolph took advantage of the moment to announce another bold step. While he had stopped the march on Washington at the crucial moment in the showdown with Roosevelt, he intended to keep the march committee alive. It would now be known as the March on Washington Movement and would be used as a sword to hang over the head of Washington's policy makers anytime they ignored the wishes of black citizens.

Randolph, now fifty-two years old, had learned the value of making controversial decisions while momentum was on his side. He now realized that World War II was rapidly stealing attention from domestic matters, including race issues.

On December 7, 1945, Japanese warplanes launched a surprise attack on the U. S. naval base at Pearl Harbor, Hawaii. President Roosevelt asked Congress to declare war on Germany and Japan the next day.

In the light of the new national emergency, some questioned whether now was the right time for a permanent Washington march movement. Even the *Amsterdam News,* which had praised Randolph so eloquently, thought his new movement could play "into the hands of Hitler and other enemies of our country and our cause."

The threat of fascism overseas put Randolph in a dilemma. He had preached against Hitler, yet had founded a movement to agitate in the United States' capital while the nation fought to stop Hitler. He decided he could not march on Washington during a time of war. Randolph's decision confused some of those loyal to the movement. How could they support a march movement that ruled out the possibility of a march?

Randolph did his best to use his newfound celebrity to keep the movement alive. He staged a series of massive, public rallies in major cities in the summer of 1942 to demonstrate that the movement could support America's fight against fascism while resisting racism at home.

An explosive case in Virginia riveted the attention of the movement. An all-white jury convicted Odell Waller, a black sharecropper, of murdering his landlord. Waller claimed that he acted in self-defense when the landlord threatened him after Waller requested a fair share of the crops he had raised. Waller told the court he needed the crops to feed his family. Nonetheless, the judge ordered that he be executed.

Randolph argued that Waller could not possibly get a fair trial because of his race and his poverty. Virginia levied a poll tax that made voting too expensive for most blacks, then used voting records to call juries. Randolph asked people to consider "whether a man convicted by a jury from which his whole economic class has been deliberately excluded can rightly be said to have been tried by a jury of his peers." The Waller case perfectly illustrated the racial injustice that Randolph turned into a major theme of the rallies. He wrote an article titled "Odell Waller Must Not Die." The title turned to a popular cry, repeated in the streets and printed on banners, building enthusiasm for the rallies.

Randolph and the Brotherhood papered Harlem with leaflets announcing the rallies as forums to address racial equality and economic justice. One of them read:

> WAKE UP, NEGRO AMERICA!
> Do you want work? Do you want equal
> rights? Do you want Justice?
> Then prepare to fight for it!

20,000 NEGROES MUST STORM
MADISON SQUARE GARDEN
MOBILIZE NOW!

The Chicago Coliseum hosted one of the early events, as did Madison Square Garden in New York. The New York rally on June 16 attracted the most attention and the greatest spectacle. Randolph wanted even those who did not attend to see the unity of the cause, so he called for Harlem businesses to dim their lights and close their doors for fifteen minutes. The *Black Worker* ran the headline "BLACK OUT HARLEM JUNE 16th." Businesses complied, rendering the streets "dark, silent and dry," in Randolph's words. Only car lights pierced the dark that night.

Twenty thousand people poured into the auditorium to hear speeches by civil rights and labor leaders. The podium was so crowded that Randolph did not even get to speak. Adam Clayton Powell Jr. of Harlem took much of the rally's spotlight when he announced that he intended to run for Congress. Powell attracted so much attention that some of Randolph's supporters grumbled he was trying to steal the show.

No one could outshine Randolph that night, though. While his close colleagues still called him "Chief," much of the public had begun referring to him as "St. Philip of the Sleeping Car Porters." He drew an ovation befitting the title when he walked into the hall surrounded by an honor guard of Pullman porters. People

shouted and called to him; before he reached the stage, the entire crowd rose to its feet. The band broke into the union anthem, "Hold the Fort for We are Coming." Randolph wrote to his old friend Owen Chandler that the Garden rally was "the biggest demonstration of Negroes in the history of the world."

Despite the spectacle, the rallies failed in one of their chief objectives. The state of Virginia executed Odell Waller on July 2, 1942. The March on Washington Movement helped organize a silent protest parade in New York on July 25. Five hundred protesters, one hundred of them white, all of them wearing black armbands, marched to the solemn echo of muffled drums.

Randolph was reminded how far America still had to go to achieve racial equality while on a speaking trip to Memphis. He planned to speak at the Mount Nemo Baptist Church, but news of Randolph's plans infuriated white political bosses. E. H. ("Boss") Crump, who ran the political machine that controlled Memphis, vowed that Randolph would not speak anywhere in the city. To drive his point home, he had the sheriff round up black preachers and drive them to the jail. Crump showed the ministers a row of empty jail cells and reminded them of what he considered the city's good treatment of its "coloreds." He told them Randolph was a rabble-rousing radical, a phony spokesman for black labor, and a dangerous advocate of racial equality. Without taking any questions from the group of black men, he then sent them home.

Opposite: The Madison Square Garden rally that Randolph organized to protest racial inequality.

Mount Nemo Baptist Church rescinded its invitation. Randolph, of course, was determined that he would find a way to speak in defiance of Boss Crump's ban. He found another church willing to host him, the First Baptist Church on Beale Street. A crowd of seven hundred showed up to hear Randolph denounce those who would silence him. He did not disappoint, calling Boss Crump a political boss "who out-Hitlers Hitler."

News of the meeting enraged Crump, but by the time he had heard about it, Randolph had already returned to New York. Crump took his anger out on Reverend G. A. Long, who had allowed Randolph to use his church. He promised to run Long out of Memphis. He made good on his promise, which stamped out the fledgling resistance to his racist power. African-American preachers tried to distance themselves from the Randolph meeting and issued a public statement: "Did the speech delivered by Randolph in which he lambasted and vilified E. H. Crump represent the attitude of the colored people of Memphis? We say NO."

The statement denouncing Randolph, which was intended to spare the preachers and their congregations from violence, did not satisfy Crump. He sent the city fire inspector to Long's church to look for "violations" of the fire code. Not surprisingly, the inspector found plenty—enough to cost $2,500 to fix. The church had only $500 in its treasury. When Randolph heard the news, he raised $2,000 from the Brotherhood and the Tennessee AFL and sent it to Long.

A sign posted near the Sojourner Truth homes, a federal housing project in Detroit, where the 1942 riots took place. *(Library of Congress)*

Racial intimidation was not confined to the South. In the summer of 1942, a year-long period of racial unrest began when a Detroit mob gathered to stop three black families from moving into a neighborhood. Resentment simmered for more than a year, and the next summer, riots broke out and spread across the country. Mob violence killed thirty-four people in Detroit and forced the government to dispatch federal troops to stop the carnage. Street fighting erupted in Harlem, Los Angeles, Mobile, and Beaumont, Texas.

A news report sparked further outrage among African Americans when a reporter revealed that German prisoners of war being transported to prisons in the South were allowed to use railroad dining cars that black soldiers, even those who guarded the prisoners, were forbidden to enter. Such incidents highlighted the prejudice experienced by black soldiers, not so much different from that suffered by their fathers and uncles in World War I.

Despite Roosevelt's order that the defense industry be integrated, the armed services were still segregated. White commanders still led all-black units. The worst jobs went to black soldiers, with three-fourths of them doing manual labor, driving trucks, and working supply lines. Even while confined to such menial jobs, they had performed some heroic feats, such as when African-American truck drivers held the Burma Road open under blistering fire from Japanese fighter planes.

Such bravery earned most black soldiers no promotions or respect. Of 776 generals, only one was black; of 5,220 colonels, seven were black. Judge William Hastie, who headed the War Department's division on policies affecting blacks, quit his job in protest of black soldiers' treatment. An African American assigned to the Pacific wrote the NAACP, saying he wanted his tombstone carved with the words "Here lies a black man killed by a yellow man fighting for the protection of the white man."

At home, lynchings of blacks continued throughout the war. The Red Cross called for blood donations, but turned away African-American donors. Fearing aerial bomb attacks like those German warplanes had rained on London, officials in Washington prepared separate bomb shelters for white and black civilians. When black soldiers tried to use the same base facilities as whites, they triggered riots at Fort Bragg, Camp Robinson, Camp Davis, Camp Lee, and Fort Dix.

When the war started, W. E. B. Du Bois had written an editorial headlined "Close Ranks!" calling for the races to stand united in the fight against fascism. Washington officials used the fear of Hitler in an effort to thwart the March on Washington Movement. "What will Berlin say?" they frequently asked Randolph and others in the movement.

But it became clear during the war years that racists in the United States did not share a desire to "close ranks." While most Americans used the "V" sign for victory, blacks began to talk about the "double V"— victory over Hitler abroad and against racism at home.

Hitler's beliefs about race, widely reported and discussed, heightened African Americans' awareness of their second-class status. Hitler believed that Nordic people were the "master race," destined to rule the world. The ideal Nordic "superman" was blond haired and blue eyed, without a trace of any other race in his bloodline. Hitler made persecution of Jews to be state policy. The Nazis beat Jews in the streets, smashed their shop windows, and sent millions to the gas chambers. Black newspapers began to question whether Nazi street thugs were so much different than the white mobs that beat and lynched black Americans. And what kind of sense did it make to fight such foes with a segregated army?

William Johnson, a painter from South Carolina who moved to New York City during the Harlem Renaissance, became famous for his depictions of daily African-American life. This work, entitled *Training for War,* is part of a series Johnson painted about the experience of black soldiers during World War II. *(Library of Congress)*

About one million African-American soldiers served during the war, a number about equal to their proportion in the population. But their white commanders, by and large, did not consider them fit for battle. Only in the winter of 1944-45, when American troops suffered severe losses at the Battle of the Bulge in Germany, did the army allow black soldiers to volunteer for infantry duty.

Black soldiers made a surprising discovery during the war, one that forever reshaped the way they considered their native country. They found that European and Asian civilians treated them better than their fellow soldiers. Many African-American soldiers could more safely walk the streets of a liberated European city than those in their own hometowns.

The war in Europe ended in April of 1945, with Germany's surrender. Japan surrendered four months later. Five hundred thousand black troops returned from overseas to find that nothing much had changed. They could not find jobs in segregated factories. Because of segregated neighborhoods, they could not use government-subsidized mortgages, a standard benefit of military service, with the same freedom as white veterans. The G.I. Bill gave financial aid to former soldiers seeking college degrees, but fewer African-American soldiers qualified because fewer had finished high school.

It reminded Randolph sadly of the situation that prevailed in the early days of *The Messenger*, when blacks fought a war for democracy only to return home to lynchings and race riots. But much had changed between the wars, as the robust rallies and demonstrations proved. Randolph would use the anger of returning soldiers as a weapon in his next battle against racism.

Eight

The Price of Democracy

World War II took some of the spotlight off racial issues, even as black soldiers returned ever more aware of racial injustice in their homeland. When the war ended, Randolph needed an issue to rekindle the movement for racial equality. The new president handed him one.

When President Roosevelt died in April of 1945, Vice President Harry Truman took office. Brash, hardheaded, and plainspoken, the former senator from Missouri inherited a changed world. The major threat to the United States now came not from Nazi Germany and militarist Japan, but from the Communist Soviet Union that had served as America's war ally. In 1947, the Soviet Union threatened to overrun Turkey and Greece. The president asked Congress for aid for both countries. He established the Truman Doctrine, which aimed to limit the influence of communism in the world and keep it contained. Thus began the Cold War, which lasted forty years.

Truman needed soldiers to keep the Soviets at bay. In 1947, he proposed a peacetime draft. The draft bill called for Universal Military Training (compulsory service for all men of a certain age), but contained no language forbidding segregation. Black soldiers would once again be asked to sacrifice for a country that refused to protect their human rights.

Randolph issued a press statement saying the draft bill was "pregnant with indecency." He joined with Grant Reynolds, Commissioner of Correction for New York State, to found the Committee Against Jim Crow in Military Service. The committee later changed its name to the League for Non-violent Civil Disobedience Against Military Segregation.

Randolph chose Bayard Rustin, who had briefly worked with him on the March on Washington Committee in 1941, to serve as executive secretary. Rustin would become Randolph's closest colleague and protégé. At thirty-eight, Rustin was tall, athletically built, and graceful, with an accent that some mistook for British. He had actually been born in West Chester, Pennsylvania. He was a former Communist who had left the party when he decided its promises to fight for African Americans were false. He was also homosexual. In an era when being black was hard enough, Rustin would have to

Bayard Rustin worked closely with Randolph during much of his career as an organizer. *(A. Philip Randolph Institute)*

battle discrimination on two fronts. His sexuality forced him to work behind the scenes of the civil rights movement for most of his life.

Rustin had first met Randolph in the late 1930s when he was still a student at City College. Rustin had no great reputation at the time and was awed by the warm reception he got from Randolph, who was known throughout America for his leadership of the Pullman Porters.

"This man of great dignity and inner beauty," Rustin later recalled, "stood up, walked from behind his desk, met me in the middle of the room, shook hands and offered me a seat." Randolph chatted amiably with his young fan, but advised him to leave the Communist party.

"I am sorry to know that you are associated with Communists because I think you're going to discover they are not interested in civil rights," Randolph said. "They are interested in using civil rights for their own purposes." When Rustin later arrived at the same conclusion, he was all the more convinced of Randolph's wisdom. Twenty years younger than Randolph, Rustin was more militant and less patient than his mentor. He sometimes grew frustrated with Randolph's deal-making approach to racial politics, preferring public protests and marches.

Randolph did drive a hard bargain in deals with white politicians, a trait he again showed in his confrontation with President Truman. When Randolph's public statements made it clear that he could make serious trouble for the president's draft bill, Truman invited him and a group of black leaders to the White House. The party included Walter White, president of the NAACP; T. Arnold Hill of the National Urban League; and Charles Houston, a special council for the NAACP.

The meeting opened with the usual pleasantries, then Randolph turned to business: "Mr. President, after making several trips around the country, I can tell you that the mood among Negroes of this country is that they will never bear arms again until all forms of bias and discrimination are abolished."

Like Randolph, Truman rarely minced words. "I wish you hadn't made that statement," he said. "I don't like it at all."

Charles Houston cut in. "But Mr. President, don't you want to know what is happening in the country?" The president had to admit that he did. On his desk sat a plaque that read "The Buck Stops Here," and he frequently complained about the yes-men that surround presidents.

"Well, that's what I'm giving you, Mr. President," Randolph continued. "I'm giving you the facts." Truman told him to go on. Randolph said, "Mr. President, as you know, we are calling upon you to issue an executive order abolishing segregation in the armed forces." When the meeting was over, Truman thanked them for coming and made no promises.

Randolph kept the pressure on Truman when he testified, nine days later, on the draft bill before the Senate Armed Services Committee.

> This time Negroes will not take a Jim Crow draft lying down. The consciousness of the world will be shaken as nothing else when thousands and thousands of us second class Americans choose imprisonment in preference to permanent military slavery. . . . I personally will advise Negroes to refuse to fight as slaves for a democracy they cannot possess and cannot enjoy. . . . I personally pledge myself to openly counsel, and abet youth, both white and Negro, to quarantine any Jim Crow conscription system whether

it bears the label of UMT [Universal Military Training]
or Selective Service.... I shall urge them to demonstrate
their solidarity with Negro youth by ignoring the
entire registration and induction machinery.

Randolph's words stunned the Senate committee. To
some, this sounded like a declaration of treason. One of
Randolph's strong supporters, Senator Wayne Morse of
Oregon, fired back at him. He described a fictional
scenario to test Randolph's conviction. "A country proceeds to attack the United States or commits acts which
make it perfectly clear that our choice is only the choice
of war," Morse said. "Would you take the position then
that unless our government granted the demands which
are set out in your testimony, or most of the demands . . .
that you would recommend a course of civil disobedience to our government?"

Randolph replied, "In the interests of the very democracy we are fighting for, I would advocate that Negroes
take no part in the Army."

Morse continued to chip at Randolph's argument,
trying to find out how far he intended to go. Did Randolph
doubt that counseling young men to disobey the law
would leave him open to a charge of treason?

Randolph answered, "I would anticipate nationwide
terrorism against Negroes but I believe that is the price
we have to pay for democracy that we want." After a few
more exchanges with Senator Morse, he admitted he
risked being charged with treason: "I would be willing
to face that doctrine on the theory and on the grounds

COMMITTEE AGAINST JIMCROW IN MILITARY SERVICE AND TRAINING

SUITE 301

217 WEST 125th STREET

NEW YORK 27, NEW YORK

Telephone: WAdsworth 6-4949

OFFICERS
Grant Reynolds
Chairman
A. Philip Randolph
Treasurer
Charles J. Patterson
Executive Secretary
LEGAL COMMITTEE
Raymond Pace Alexander
Sadie T. M. Alexander
Matthew W. Bullock, Jr.
Robert L. Carter
Earl B. Dickerson
Charles H. Houston
Belford V. Lawson, Jr.
James M. Nabrit

July 15, 1948

President Harry S. Truman
White House
Washington, D. C.

Dear Mr. President:

We were indeed happy that you decided to call Congress back into special session in order to act on civil rights legislation, among other matters. We trust that in your message to Congress on July 26 you will specifically ask for legislative approval of anti-lynching and other safeguards for Negro draftees. You are undoubtedly aware of the intense bitterness on the part of Negro citizens because of the bi-partisan "gentlemen's agreement" to scuttle the Langer amendments to the draft bill early in June.

The action most necessary today to strengthen the fabric of democracy is of the type that would enhance the dignity of second-class citizens. Because the 1948 Republican platform expressed its disapproval of army segregation and because the recently adopted platform of your own party in essence called for the abolition of racial distinctions within the military establishment, we feel that you now have a bi-partisan mandate to end military segregation forthwith by the issuance of an Executive Order.

May we take this opportunity to renew our request for a conference with you in the immediate future to discuss such an Executive Order. The date for registration under the draft is only a month away and it is the hope of all Negro youth that there will be an alternative beyond submission to a discriminatory law and imprisonment for following the dictates of self-respect.

Sincerely,

Grant Reynolds, National Chairman

A. Philip Randolph, National Treasurer

GR/k

A letter to President Truman from Reynolds and Randolph asking for a meeting to discuss an executive order banning discrimination in the military. *(National Archives)*

that we are serving a higher law than the law which applies the act of treason to us when we are attempting to win democracy in this country and to make the soul of America democratic."

If African Americans did not get equal treatment, then America was not a free society, Randolph insisted. Dis-

Grant Reynolds and A. Philip Randolph testify before the Senate Armed Forces Committee. *(Library of Congress)*

obeying the law would be "the only way by which we are going to make America wake up and realize that we do not have democracy here as long as one black man in the country is denied all of the rights enjoyed by all the white men in this country."

The senators, including his ally Morse, were convinced that they were listening to a very dangerous man. Outside the Senate, Randolph dropped the elevated language he had used in the hearing and spoke his message plainly to a waiting crowd of supporters. "I am prepared to oppose a Jim Crow army till I rot in jail," he said.

Press reaction to Randolph's strong words before the Senate committee was mixed. One white journalist described his testimony as "one of the most impressive and courageous statements that has ever been made before a Congressional Committee by any man, white or black." But most newspapers considered his stand far too dangerous, as did the *New York World-Telegram* when it said Randolph and his supporters had done "their race and their country a great disservice."

A writer for the *Black Worker* wrote to the *World-Telegram* in response to its charges: "Like most white individuals or organizations you cannot understand the thinking or test the pulse of the Negro people . . . Greater is the fear of most Negroes in serving or training in the armed services in the Southern sections of this country than that experienced on the firing lines facing a foreign enemy."

Black people offered Randolph more support than most newspapers did. A poll of black New Yorkers found that the majority agreed with him, at least as long as the country was at peace. Seven of ten black college students stood with Randolph, according to another poll.

Randolph used the League for Non-Violent Civil Disobedience Against Military Segregation as a counter force against the Universal Military Training bill. Volunteers got young men to sign pledges that they would not serve in a segregated military force. They handed out leaflets in Harlem and set up street corner tables with petitions against the draft. They drove trucks with megaphones playing jazz music through black neighborhoods, attracting people's attention, and then delivering short speeches against the Jim Crow military.

Randolph called public rallies, honing and refining

the message that he had delivered spontaneously to the first crowd he met after testifying. "We will fill up the jails with young men who refuse to serve," he said. "And I am prepared to fight the Jim Crow army even if I am convicted of treason and have to rot in jail. The time has come when we can no longer fight under the flag of segregation. We will no longer give aid and comfort to our enemies."

But he also warned black men they would be taking a dangerous position if they followed him: "If you refuse to be drafted, you must be prepared to go to jail. We are fighting to pressure the President into issuing an executive order banning discrimination in the armed forces. Think carefully about what you do, because when we get our executive order, we will have achieved our goals and will disband. You may have to remain in prison. It is a tremendous sacrifice, so think about it. But if you decide to do it, you will be helping all black people take a step closer to freedom."

The NAACP refused to counsel young men to avoid the draft, but its secretary, Walter White, defended the spirit of Randolph's testimony. "We would have valiant allies," he wrote Senator Morse, "if you and some of your allies in the Senate could darken your faces and serve in uniform for six weeks."

Congressman Adam Clayton Powell warned his colleagues in the Senate that they could not afford to ignore Randolph's words. He said Randolph "did most emphatically state the mood of the vast majority of the fifteen

million colored Americans. He did not overstate it. . .
. We are not going to be frightened by the cry of 'Treason.' If the finger of treason can be pointed at anyone,
it must be pointed at you who are traitors to our Con-
stitution and to our Bill of Rights. There aren't enough
jails in America to hold the colored people who will
refuse to bear arms in a Jim Crow army."

The situation for President Truman grew politically
dangerous as the summer of 1948 approached. He needed
the support of African-American voters to win the up-
coming election. Randolph kept the issue at a boiling
point. In July, when the Democrats held their political
convention, a ring of black protesters surrounded their
Philadelphia convention hall. Randolph himself carried
a protest sign reading, "PRISON IS BETTER THAN
ARMY JIM CROW SERVICE."

Truman finally realized he could not preserve a Jim
Crow draft. On July 26, he issued Executive Order 9981,
which stated, "there shall be equality of treatment and
opportunity for all persons in the armed services without regard to race, color, religion, or national origin. This
policy shall be put into effect as rapidly as possible."

But as President Roosevelt had learned, Randolph
would not call off a fight if he was not satisfied that his
adversary's concession would produce results. Randolph
found it disturbing that the executive order did not
include the word "segregation." He demanded that President Truman clarify the point. Truman sent word through

Opposite: Randolph, left, marches at the Democratic National Convention in
Chicago.

a congressman that segregation would no longer be tolerated. Satisfied, Randolph telegraphed his congratulations to the president and prepared to dismantle the anti-draft campaign.

For the second time in seven years, Randolph had forced an American president to back down. It was one of the great achievements of black civil rights in the twentieth century. But his younger, more militant followers, including Bayard Rustin, didn't see it that way. They still did not think the wording was strong enough.

There was another issue as well. Some men had followed Randolph's advice to resist the draft and gone to jail for it. Rustin and others raised the point when Randolph called them in to disband the committee. "I'm sorry," Randolph replied. "Those men knew the risks they were taking. We made a solemn pledge that when an executive order is issued, we would disband."

Randolph ordered Rustin to set up a press conference announcing his decision. Rustin reluctantly did so, but decided to sabotage his mentor's message. He set the press conference for four in the afternoon. He then called a press conference for the young dissenters in Randolph's camp for ten in the morning. The young radicals called the executive order a "weasly worded, mealy mouthed sham" and denounced Randolph for accepting it. By the time Randolph took the podium to make his own statement, the afternoon papers had already published the remarks of his discontented followers.

The young radicals had underestimated the strength of the order. President Truman stuck by his promise to end Jim Crow in the military. He told a committee called to enforce the order, "If I have to knock some heads together to get the action you need, I'll knock some heads together." By 1954, the army was fully integrated.

Bayard Rustin came to realize that he and the other dissidents had been wrong. He later admitted his shame at sabotaging Randolph's press conference. Two years later, he decided to go to the older man and apologize. When Randolph welcomed Rustin into his office, Rustin was as surprised at his graciousness as he had been at their first meeting.

"Why Bayard," Randolph said, "where have you been? You know I needed you." The two men thereafter worked together as allies for the rest of their lives.

Randolph was always quick to forgive, partly because he knew he could never win the racial struggle alone. He needed Rustin's organizational skills for battles yet to come, including the long-awaited Washington march for freedom.

Nine

March on Washington

The labor leaders who had resisted Randolph's early calls for the desegregation of unions gradually began to see the justice of his cause. When the AFL and CIO merged in 1955, their members elected him to sit on the executive council. In 1957, he became vice president. By the late 1950s, most unions accepted black members. Randolph continued, however, to speak out against the few unions that remained segregated.

Though many labor leaders agreed with his position, they were sometimes exasperated by his steadfastness. When Randolph demanded that the organization expel the all-white Brotherhood of Railroad Firemen and Brotherhood of Railroad Trainmen if they did not integrate, AFL-CIO President George Meany lost his temper.

"Who the hell appointed you guardian of all the

Negroes in America?" the red-faced Meany shouted. By this time, it was quite clear to most African Americans that Randolph deserved his position as a black union spokesman. Newspapers joined black leaders in criticizing the remarks. Meany later reversed his position and declared his determination to root

George Meany. *(Library of Congress)*

out the "last vestiges of discrimination in the labor movement." The AFL-CIO staunchly supported the civil rights struggle of the 1960s.

The black civil rights movement began to achieve victories that Randolph could only dream of when his fiery editorials in *The Messenger* earned him the reputation of a radical. In 1954, the Supreme Court ruled school segregation illegal in the landmark *Brown v. Board of Education* case.

The momentum for racial equality seemed to grow year by year. In December of 1955, black seamstress and NAACP worker Rosa Parks refused to take a seat in the back of a bus in Montgomery, Alabama. When she was arrested, black leaders in Montgomery staged a boycott of the buses. Dr. Martin Luther King led the movement against the bus lines. King, twenty-six, was pastor of the Dexter Avenue Baptist Church. Youthful, charismatic, and eloquent, King inspired crowds with speeches that borrowed the phrases and rhythms of the pulpit. In years to come, King's reputation would grow and come to overshadow Randolph as the most prominent black leader in America.

Randolph nonetheless remained an energetic spokesman for the cause of racial equality and justice. He turned sixty-one in 1950, but looked and acted like he

On the stage at the prayer pilgrimage on May 17, 1957. *From left to right:* Roy Wilkins, Randolph, Thomas Kilgore, Martin Luther King Jr. *(Library of Congress)*

was twenty years younger. In 1957, he led a civil rights march to Washington called the Prayer Pilgrimage. The next year he led the Youth March for Integrated Schools, an event that drew 10,000 people, along with such celebrities as baseball star Jackie Robinson and singer Harry Belafonte.

Bayard Rustin remained Randolph's closest confidante, even as he advised King on tactics for the Montgomery boycott. On a winter day in 1962, the two men sat in a Harlem office and talked over some of the inequalities that African Americans still suffered. The black unemployment rate, for example, remained considerably higher than that for whites. The one-hundredth anniversary of President Abraham Lincoln's Emancipation Proclamation, the document that freed American slaves in the south, was coming up in 1963. Randolph suggested an Emancipation March on Washington, with every major civil rights organization in the country taking part. Rustin eagerly embraced the idea, and Randolph appointed him to organize it.

They quickly got commitments to join from leaders of other movements, including James Farmer of the Congress of Racial Equality and John Lewis of the Student Nonviolent Coordinating Committee. King agreed to join, but wanted the name changed to the March on Washington for Jobs and Freedom. Rustin and Randolph agreed. The date was set for August 28, 1963.

A terrible tragedy struck Randolph during the planning for the march. His wife, Lucille, who had been confined to a wheelchair for ten years after being crippled by arthritis, died on April 12, 1963. Since they had no children, her death left Randolph alone. His only solace came from his work preparing for a march she had not lived to see.

News of the march worried President John F. Kennedy. A bloody riot in Birmingham, Alabama, that spring had already raised the level of racial tension in America. Birmingham police had attacked a desegregation march led by King. Television cameras captured one violent scene after another, as officers of police chief Bull Connor turned fire hoses on the marchers, set attack dogs on them and shocked them with cattle prods.

Like most Americans, the president had watched the horrifying spectacle on television. The planners of the March on Washington had promised their event would be nonviolent, but Kennedy feared their racist opponents might not be so peaceful. He summoned the leaders of the march to the White House.

President Kennedy always seemed amiable and charming before crowds and on television, but appeared ill at ease when Randolph and the others came into his office. This was apparently not a meeting he wanted to have.

Kennedy told them he preferred the march not take place. The mood could turn ugly, as it had in Birmingham. It could even endanger civil rights legislation currently before Congress. The president's arguments did not sway Randolph. "Mr. President, the masses are restless," he said. "We are going to march on Washington."

"Mr. Randolph," President Kennedy said, "if you bring all these people to Washington, won't that bring violence and a great deal of disorder?"

Randolph answered, "Mr. President, this will be an orderly, peaceful, nonviolent demonstration."

The president still seemed uncomfortable. "I think we have some problems here," he said and left the room, leaving the meeting in the hands of his brother, Attorney General Robert Kennedy, and Vice President Lyndon Johnson. The meeting with Kennedy was the tensest White House meeting Randolph had gone through.

As political negotiations continued, Rustin worked behind the scenes on a task that few other organizers could have handled. He took charge of overseeing the thousand little details that went into any mass event, such as finding transportation, food, water, lodging, and even toilets for the marchers. He worked out of an office in Harlem, chain-smoking cigarettes as he talked on the phone to reporters and heads of other civil rights groups. His small staff made sixteen-hour days routine as they printed manuals, wrote releases, stuffed envelopes, and mapped travel routes. He wanted to mass a crowd of 250,000, but kept the target number secret from the press. Rustin told reporters to expect 100,000 marchers, to prevent the movement from being embarrassed should the turnout be disappointing.

An ardent enemy of the civil rights movement tried to use Rustin's homosexuality to halt the march. Senator Strom Thurmond of South Carolina, one of the nation's

Bayard Rustin works behind the scenes at the organizing offices for the March on Washington. *(Courtesy of Getty Images.)*

most fervent segregationists, made Rustin's homosexuality public on the Senate floor just two weeks before the event. Thurmond had a potent weapon in his arsenal: Rustin's 1953 arrest record for a sexual encounter with two men in Pasadena, California.

The charge against Rustin bore the ominous title of "sex perversion," and it triggered sensational national headlines. Pressure mounted for Rustin to resign, but Randolph intervened to save his efficient right-hand man. Randolph returned from a conference with labor leaders and held a press conference in New York. "I speak for the combined Negro leadership," he said, "in voicing my complete confidence in Bayard Rustin's character . . . I am dismayed that there are in this country men who, wrapping themselves in the mantle of Christian morality, would mutilate the most elementary conceptions of human decency, privacy and humility in order to attack other men."

Randolph's staunch defense of Rustin put his own reputation on the line, but it worked. In part because Randolph had confronted the issue head-on, the story faded into the background as newspapers and television returned to coverage of the march itself.

The biggest question was whether the march would draw anything near the numbers its organizers had promised. When the day arrived, Randolph and Rustin had their doubts. The streets of Washington, D.C., were almost empty in the early morning of August 28, 1963.

One reason was fear. The march's opponents had done a good job of convincing Washington's citizens that they might see another Birmingham play out in their streets. Thousands of city residents stayed home from work. Some had left the city to stay with friends or relatives. Even members of Congress had found excuses to leave the capital.

But the reporters and photographers showed up in hordes. By six AM, they had gathered around Rustin, demanding to know where the crowds were. He pretended to be calm, assuring them that everything was going according to plan.

By nine-thirty, 40,000 demonstrators had arrived at the monument. In an hour, the crowd doubled. Before noon, the march surged well beyond the conservative estimates, with more than 250,000 gathered in Washington's streets. Hollywood celebrities such as Marlon Brando, Paul Newman, Sydney Poitier, and Charlton Heston marched onto the mall, as did folk singers Joan Baez and Bob Dylan.

The marchers' procession to the Lincoln Memorial began at about noon. They carried picket signs with such slogans as "Equal Rights NOW," "Jobs for All NOW," "Integrated Schools NOW," "Voting Rights NOW," and "Freedom Rights, NOW."

Organizers of the march join the energized crowd as they process to the Lincoln Memorial. Randolph is at the center of this photograph. *(National Archives)*

Randolph delivered the keynote address, the last major speech of his life. "Let the nation and the world know the meaning of our numbers," he declared. "We are not a pressure group , we are not an organization or a group of organizations, we are not a mob. We are the advance guard of a massive moral revolution for jobs and freedom. . . . But this civil rights revolution is not confined to the Negro, nor is it confined to civil rights, for our white allies know they cannot be free while we are not, and we know we have no future in a society in which six million black and white people are unemployed and millions live in poverty."

Randolph hammered the theme of jobs, while denouncing those who would let racism prevail in the name of "law and order." He declared, "It falls to us to demand full employment and to put automation at the service of human needs, not at the service of profits. . . . All who deplore our militancy, who exhort patience in the name of false peace, are in fact supporting segregation and exploitation. They would have social peace at the expense of social and racial justice. They are more concerned with easing racial tensions than enforcing racial democracy."

After introducing the many speakers, Randolph brought Dr. King to the podium, praising him as "the man who personifies the moral leadership of the civil rights revolution." The organizers had placed King last because they knew he would give a good speech and people would wait for the chance to hear him.

Overleaf: Crowds filled the Mall on August 28, 1963, for the March on Washington. *(National Archives)*

King did not disappoint. Departing from his prepared text when he delivered an extemporaneous line or two from the Bible, and heard cheers from the crowd, King decided to speak from the heart. The result was his historic "I Have a Dream" address, in which he talked about his dream of an America that knew no color barriers. He sounded more like a preacher than a radical when he shouted out his vision of an America that sounded like heaven, especially to African Americans:

> I have a dream that one day this nation will rise up to live out the true meaning of its creed: "We hold these truths to be self evident; that all men are created equal!" I have a dream that one day on the red hills of Georgia the sons of former slaves and the sons of former slave-holders will be able to sit down together at the table of brotherhood. I have a dream that one day even the state of Mississippi, a desert state sweltering with the heat of injustice and oppression, will be transformed into an oasis of freedom and justice. I have a dream that my four little children will one day live in a nation where they will not be judged by the color of their skin but the content of their character. I have a dream today.

The repeated refrain had a galvanizing effect as the 250,000 marchers cheered every repetition of the words "I have a dream." King's final words declared a deliverance from oppression with the words "Free at last! Free at last! Thank God Almighty, we are free at last!"

Randolph closed the march by leading a pledge that called for the marchers to continue to fight for racial justice until victory was won. The giant crowd spoke with one voice, saying "I do so pledge . . ." President Kennedy heard the tumultuous crowd through the windows of the White House as he watched it on the television screen. He also listened as the crowd sang the song that had become the hymn of the civil rights movement: "We Shall Overcome."

The president was relieved that the march, as promised, produced no violence. He later received Randolph and the other leaders at the White House, congratulated them, and promised to work toward passing more civil rights legislation through Congress.

The organizers meet with President Kennedy at the White House. Randolph is at the center, next to Kennedy. Martin Luther King Jr. is third from the left. *(National Archives)*

March organizers gather at the Lincoln Memorial after the event. *From left to right:* Mathew Ahmann, Cleveland Robinson, Rabbi Joachim Prinz, A. Philip Randolph, Joseph Rauh Jr., John Lewis, and Floyd McKissick. *(National Archives)*

The march had changed the course of history in one day. Randolph had spent his life in battles that usually consisted of meetings and negotiations, often accompanied by threats. The March on Washington was different. It provided a note of glorious pageantry that succeeded in part because millions saw it on television. In many ways, it was the proudest day of the civil rights movement.

As sunset neared, Randolph stood by the Lincoln Memorial watching the crowd leave for the buses, cars, and trains that would take them home. Bayard Rustin abandoned the street cleaning crews for a few minutes to talk with his old mentor.

"Mr. Randolph," he said, "it looks like your dream has come true." Randolph was known for keeping his emotions in check, but at that moment tears streamed down his cheeks.

Although many members of Congress had not been in town for the March on Washington, its impact had not been lost on them. President Kennedy would not pass any further civil rights legislation, for he would not live out the year. On November 22, 1963, an assassin gunned down the president in Dallas, Texas. But under President Lyndon Johnson, a civil rights bill was passed in 1964 that barred discrimination in public places such as restaurants and hotels, gave the government more power to fight school segregation, and ended discrimination in federally funded programs, including prejudice in hiring. The next year, the Voting Rights Act ensured that states could take no steps to bar blacks from voting.

Randolph had made a career fighting Washington officials and presidents who used every political trick to stall, hinder, and slow the progress of civil rights. He had grown tired of half-measures. The changes that came in the wake of the march proved him right in predicting the nation would heed "the meaning of our numbers."

Ten

The Turning Point

So many public accolades and congratulations poured down on Randolph after the March on Washington that younger people might never have suspected he was once called "the most dangerous Negro in America." Many of his once "radical" views had become mainstream American values, the simple standards of common decency between the races.

His picture, along with that of his loyal disciple Bayard Rustin, appeared on the cover of *Life* magazine the month following the march. The irony must have seemed particularly striking to the older man. In his early days, even the black press had frequently denounced him as too extreme. Now his face appeared on the main coffee table publication in the nation, depicting him as an elder statesman of civil rights.

Rustin and Randolph on the cover of *Life* magazine, September 6, 1963.

The march would be celebrated as the symbol of a turning point in American racial history. It stamped the civil rights movement with a spirit of optimism, highlighted by the lyrical King speech and the strains of "We Shall Overcome." A year later, President Johnson awarded Randolph the prestigious Medal of Freedom.

Unfortunately, the struggle was far from over. Waves of violence shook the nation throughout the 1960s, beginning almost on the heels of the march. On September 15, 1963, a bomb blast at a church in Birmingham killed four young black girls. Barely more than a month later, Lee Harvey Oswald killed President Kennedy. The decade marked a time of great progress, but also of brutal bloodshed.

Although he was in his 70s, Randolph did not want to retire from racial activism at such an important time. He and Rustin established the A. Philip Randolph Institute in 1964. The institute attempted to use political means to implement Randolph's central ideas, such as his economic view of the racial divide, liberal solutions for social problems, and full integration of labor unions.

The AFL-CIO buried its past disagreements with Randolph and became a major contributor to the organization. When the Randolph Institute sought to orga-

Randolph accepts the Medal of Freedom from Lyndon Johnson. *(Library of Congress)*

nize black trade union members to get out the vote, the AFL-CIO's Committee on Political Education (COPE) pitched in to help. The AFL-CIO's Civil Rights Department worked closely with Randolph's organization to desegregate construction unions, one of the last holdouts in excluding black workers. The unions and the institute worked together to establish apprenticeship programs to bring black and Puerto Rican workers into the construction industry.

AFL-CIO President George Meany, who had often argued so furiously with Randolph in the 1950s, called his organization's contributions to the Randolph Institute "one of the best investments" it had ever made.

Randolph got more cooperation from President Johnson than any of his predecessors in the White House. Johnson appointed him honorary chairman of the White House Conference on Civil Rights in 1966. "In the near future, I shall call upon the leaders of the Freedom Movement to meet together with economists and social scientists in order to work out a specific and documented 'Freedom Budget,'" he said at the first meeting.

Randolph followed through on his promise. He directed the Randolph Institute to research a plan for economic equality, then got more than two hundred prominent citizens and civil rights groups to pledge their support. The Institute issued the "Freedom Budget for All Americans" in 1966. It called for a ten-year plan to wipe out poverty, clean up slums, provide jobs at decent wages, bring the economy to full production, and clean up the environment.

The sticking point for some of Randolph's critics was the price tag. The budget would have required $185 billion over ten years. Randolph argued that the money was not an expenditure, but an investment. "The question is not whether we have the means," he said. "The question is whether we have the will. Ten years from now, will two-fifths of our nation still live in poverty and deprivation? This is, above all, a moral question. And upon the answer hangs not only the fate of the Negro—weighed down by centuries of exploitation, degradation and malice—but the fate of the nation." Despite Randolph's appeals, the Freedom Budget was deemed too costly and never approved.

The Randolph Institute provided Randolph with a modest salary, the steadiest income he had earned in a life of activism. That was one of Rustin's goals when he set up the organization. Randolph nonetheless remained indifferent to financial rewards for his own work. Chandler Owen, his old co-editor from *The Messenger* days, tried in vain to get Randolph to use his prestige to build some financial security. Owen urged Randolph to write his memoirs, which Owen would promote as a screenplay for the movies. Randolph refused, although he granted interviews freely to other biographers. Owen also tried to get Randolph to let him set up an organization to support him financially, as admirers of W. E. B. Du Bois and Booker T. Washington had done.

"I am sure you know that I have no money and, at the same time, don't expect to get any," Randolph wrote Owen. "However, I would not think of having a movement started to raise money for me and my family. It is the lot of some people to be poor and it is my lot, which I do not have any remorse about. Besides, I am not in need of any bread [money], but even if I were, I would not wish a movement to help me get any."

Undaunted, Owen came up with another idea. He wanted to rally support for getting Randolph the Nobel Prize for Peace, mainly for the $40,000 of tax-free income it would bring. "You are the world's greatest peace maker," he wrote his old friend. "As head of the march on Washington, you are the world's greatest peace producer." Randolph refused to permit any such campaign. Owen finally gave up trying to help his old friend with money. In November of 1967, Owen died of a kidney ailment.

Younger black leaders became more militant as the decade rolled on. Randolph did not always support them, and even disagreed with their harsher rhetoric. But he did understand how they felt, because he still remembered the anger of his own youth and his lifelong battle with authority.

Stokely Carmichael, director of the Student Nonviolent Coordinating Committee, introduced a new word to the language of racial politics at a rally in Greenwood, Mississippi, in 1966. "What we are going to start saying now is 'Black Power,'" Carmichael said. He meant the phrase as a more militant alternative to the "Freedom Now" slogan carried on the signs of the earliest marchers. He led his audience through chants of "Black Power! Black Power!"

The phrase took hold in the media and became a battle cry for black radicals. The Black Power movement preached self-defense and black separatism, much as Marcus Garvey had during the 1920s. The call for Black Power led to the establishment of the Black Panthers, who called for an armed revolution against the white power structure.

Randolph thought violence entirely unnecessary for the civil rights movement. The militants were quick to label him an "Uncle Tom" because of his pacifism. He was nowhere near as quick to condemn them.

Stokely Carmichael, photographed here at age twenty-five, was the head of the Student Nonviolent Coordinating Committee. He introduced the phrase "Black Power" to the civil rights movement. *(AP Photo)*

"I think they [the militants] have been instrumental in turning America around and giving it a sense of the danger of the grave crisis in the cities," he told a CBS interviewer. "They deserve that credit. I don't agree with their methods but they have a romance in their hearts for freedom. Victims of great oppression, youngsters who have dreams for a better future, they remind me of my own self in the '20s."

The violence of the middle to late 1960s played into the militants' hands. The nation's involvement in the unpopular Vietnam War created protests in the streets, often marred by clashes with police. Malcolm X, a radical of the Black Muslim group, urged separation of the races and violent overthrow of white rule. He had just begun to moderate his message, seeking greater reconciliation with white society, when he was gunned down in 1965. On April 4, 1968, an assassin shot Dr. Martin Luther King dead as he stood on the balcony of a Memphis motel. Riots broke out in more than one hundred U.S. cities.

While Randolph understood the feelings of black radicals, he also thought rioting damaged the civil rights movement. He called for young African Americans to improve their lot through education, sounding far ahead of his time when he urged them to improve their technology skills.

"The youngsters of today must direct their attention not only to the matter of racial identity and racial realization through African studies, but they must make certain they are not left behind in the scientific and technological revolution, because if they are, they will be in a hopeless state," he said. "There will be absolutely no way in the world whereby they can become an effective force. If the young Negro can't become a part of this advancing technology, his whole revolution will have been in vain."

Although he still waded into the thick of almost every public debate, Randolph's friends noticed that he was becoming more frail. In 1968, he attended his last meeting of the Brotherhood of Sleeping Car Porters and resigned as its president.

Randolph spent more time in his Ninth Avenue apartment, reading, answering the phone, and giving interviews, but rarely calling anyone himself. He developed a heart ailment that caused dizzy spells and sometimes made him collapse on the floor. When his doctor advised physical exercise, he began exercising at seven-thirty every morning in his bedroom and jogging laps around his apartment.

Bayard Rustin took it upon himself to aid Randolph. Visitors saw Rustin helping the older man with his meals, cutting his meat into small pieces as he ate. Like a son, Rustin had fallen out with the older man during his own youth, but reconciled as they both grew older. He never forgot the way Randolph put his own reputation on the line during Senator Strom Thurmond's smear campaign.

In 1969, Randolph celebrated his eightieth birthday. Thirteen hundred of the most prominent people in America

Coretta Scott King, Martin Luther King Jr.'s widow, congratulates Randolph at his eightieth birthday party. Bayard Rustin and George Meany stand to Coretta King's right. *(Library of Congress)*

turned out for the dinner at the Waldorf-Astoria Hotel. New York governor Nelson Rockefeller attended, as did George Meany of the AFL-CIO, Roy Wilkins of the NAACP, and Dr. King's widow, Coretta Scott King. One speaker after another stood to praise Randolph's achievements.

Bayard Rustin rose to say that, except for his grandparents, "no one has stood beside me in times of trial the way Mr. Randolph has. He is the only man I know who has never said an unkind word about anyone, or who refuses to listen to an unkind word about anyone, even though it may be true. I've known him all these years, and I still can't bring myself to address him in any other way but as 'Mr. Randolph.'"

Roy Wilkins praised him as an inspiration to young people. "When I came along as a young man, you were my hero, my inspiration. You caught me at a time when every young college boy should be caught—when he is full of idealism and when he believes that the world can be changed. And here was a man changing it, who was confident it could be changed, who never faltered, who never gave his followers anything but the hope of victory."

Asa Philip Randolph lived quietly during the last decade of his life. As younger civil rights leaders took up the cause, his fame dimmed for the current generation. On his infrequent walks in the city, not as many people recognized him as in the past. He died on May 16, 1979, at the age of ninety.

The eulogies following his death made it clear that history would not forget him. The news stories pointed out that he had been a pioneer of the civil rights movement who had fought to break down racial barriers decades before the modern civil rights era was born. Asa Philip Randolph touched hundreds of thousands of people in his career, from the Jim Crow 1920s to the turbulent 1960s, inspiring both white and black Americans on the long march to justice.

Timeline

1889   Born in Crescent City, Florida, on April 15.´

1907   Graduates from Cookman Institute.

1911   Leaves Jacksonville for Harlem; enrolls in City College.

1914   Marries Lucille Campbell Green.

1917   With Chandler Owen, founds *The Messenger*.

1925   Founds and becomes first president of the Brotherhood of Sleeping Car Porters.

1937   Pullman Company signs agreement with Brotherhood, raising wages and shortening hours.

1941   Threatens national march on Washington to protest segregation of military and hiring discrimination; meets with President Franklin Delano Roosevelt; Roosevelt issues executive order banning discrimination in government or hiring in defense plants.

1943   Holds massive rallies to protest racial inequality, including event at Madison Square Garden.

1948   Threatens march on Washington to protest segregation of military; meets with President Harry Truman; Truman issues executive order ending military segregation.

1957   Becomes vice president of AFL-CIO.

1963   Leads March for Jobs and Freedom in Washington.

1964   Awarded Medal of Freedom by President Lyndon Johnson; establishes A. Philip Randolph Institute.

1968   Attends last meeting of Brotherhood of Sleeping Car Porters, resigns as president.

1979   Dies at the age of ninety, on May 16.

Sources

Chapter One: Pride Against Prejudice

p. 12, "We understand that . . ." Jervis Anderson, *A. Philip Randolph: A Biographical Portrait* (New York: Harcourt Brace Jovanovich, Inc., 1972), 29.

p. 15, "a nose, a chin . . ." Ibid., 36.

p. 16, "If the church . . ." Ibid., 37.

p. 18, "two of the finest . . ." Ibid., 40.

p. 18-19, "Get the hell . . ." Ibid., 41.

p. 22, "I was important . . ." Ibid., 47.

Chapter Two: Street Radical

p. 29, "the only thing . . ." Robert H. Brisbane, *The Black Vanguard: Origins of the Negro Social Revolution 1900-1960* (Valley Forge: Judson Press, 1970), 51.

Chapter Three: Dangerous Men

p. 43-44, "those who . . ." Anderson, *A. Philip Randolph*, 97.

p. 44-45, "We of the . . ." Ibid., 99.

p. 45, "Since when has . . ." Ibid., 101.

p. 46, "Those two American . . ." Daniel S. Davis, *Mr. Black Labor: The Story of A. Philip Randolph, Father of the Civil Rights Movement* (New York: E.P. Dutton & Co., Inc., 1972), 20.

p. 46, "preaching the gospel . . ." Ibid., 19.

p. 48, "A certain class . . ." Ibid., 24.

p. 48, "the most dangerous . . ." Anderson, *A. Philip Randolph*, 108.

p. 49, "by long odds . . ." Paula F. Pfeffer, *A. Philip Randolph: Pioneer of the Civil Rights Movement* (Baton Rouge and London: Lousiana State University Press, 1990), 18.

p. 50, "little fat black . . ." Robert H. Brisbane, *The Black Vanguard: Origins of the Negro Social Revolution, 1900-1960* (Valley Forge, Judson Press, 1970), 85.

p. 52, "There's a young . . . Africa ourselves" Anderson, *A. Philip Randolph,* 122.

p. 52, "I could tell . . ." Ibid., 130.

Chapter Four: Building the Brotherhood

p. 62, "I am not . . ." Pffefer, *A. Philip Randolph,* 21.

p. 63, "I told the . . ." Anderson, *A. Philip Randolph,* 169.

p. 63, "At the end . . ." Ibid.

p. 65, "all the crooks . . ." Ibid., 170.

p. 66, "knew that slanderers . . ." Davis, *Mr. Black Labor,* 55.

p. 66-67, "This movement is . . ." Ibid., 59.

p. 69, "next to the . . ." Anderson, *A. Philip Randolph,* 203.

Chapter Five: Porter versus Pullman

p. 70, "nothing can keep . . ." Anderson, *A. Philip Randolph,* 215.

p. 72, "pay the price . . ." Ibid., 207.

p. 75, "There is no . . ." Davis, *Mr. Black Labor,* 75.

p. 76, "We had no . . ." Anderson, *A. Philip Randolph,* 221.

p. 76-77, "Here was this . . ." Ibid.

p. 77, "He said 'C. L. . . .'" Ibid., 223.

p. 79, "People we never . . ." Ibid., 227.

p. 81, "unsound, defenseless . . ." Davis, *Mr. Black Labor,* 84.

p. 81-82, "The American Federation . . ." Ibid., 85.

Chapter Six: The President's Order

p. 84, "We have not had . . ." Davis, *Mr. Black Labor,* 100.

p. 84, "Labor has been . . ." Anderson, *A. Philip Randolph*, 242.

p. 85, "Of equal importance . . ." Ibid.

p. 87, "the policy of . . ." Ibid., 244.

p. 88, "You know, Web . . . I think we can get them." Ibid., 247.

p, 89, "In this period . . ." Davis, *Mr. Black Labor*, 104.

p. 89-90, "The Negroes stake . . ." Ibid.

p. 90, "This is the . . ." Pfeffer, *A. Philip Randolph*, 47.

p. 94-95, "Mr. President, time . . . hundred thousand, Mr. President," Anderson, *A. Philip Randolph*, 257.

p. 95-96, "there shall be no . . ." Davis, *Mr. Black Labor*, 130.

p. 96, "Who is this guy . . ." Anderson, *A. Philip Randolph*, 259.

Chapter Seven: The Double V

p. 97, "A. Philip Randolph . . ." Davis, *Mr. Black Labor*, 112.

p. 98, "the most astonishing . . ." Anderson, *A. Philip Randolph*, 262.

p. 98, "a kind of . . ." Ibid.

p. 99, "into the hands . . ." Ibid., 264.

p. 100, "whether a man . . ." Pfeffer, *A. Philip Randolph*, 77.

p. 100-101, "WAKE UP, NEGRO . . ." Davis, *Mr. Black Labor*, 118.

p. 101, "BLACK OUT HARLEM . . ." Ibid.

p. 101, "dark, silent and . . ." Anderson, *A. Philip Randolph*, 264.

p. 103, "the biggest demonstration . . ." Ibid., 265.

p. 104, "who out-Hitlers ..." Ibid., 270.

p. 104, "Did the speech . . ." Ibid.

p. 106, "Here lies a . . ." Davis, *Mr. Black Labor*, 122.

p. 107, "What will Berlin . . ." Robert W. Mullen, *Blacks in America's Wars* (Pathfinder: New York, London, Montreal, Sydney, 1973), 55.

Chapter Eight: The Price of Democracy

p. 111, "pregnant with indecency," Anderson, *A. Philip Randolph*, 274.

p. 112-113, "This man of . . ." John D'Emilio, *Lost Prophet: The Life and Times of Bayard Rustin* (New York, London, Toronto, Sydney, Singapore: Free Press, 2003), 58.

p. 113, "I am sorry . . ." James Haskins, *Bayard Rustin: Behind the Scenes of the Civil Rights Movement* (New York: Hyperion Books for Children, 1997), 21.

p. 113-114, "Mr. President, after . . . segregation in the armed forces," Anderson, *A. Philip Randolph*, 276.

p. 114-115, "This time Negroes . . ." Ibid.

p. 115, "A country proceeds . . ." Ibid., 277.

p. 115, "In the interests . . ." Ibid.

p. 115, "I would anticipate . . ." Ibid.

p. 116, "I would be . . ." Ibid.

p. 117, "the only way . . ." Mullen, *Blacks in America's Wars*, 59.

p. 117, "I am prepared . . ." Anderson, *A. Philip Randolph*, 278.

p. 118, "one of the . . ." Pfeffer, *A. Philip Randolph*, 144.

p. 118, "their race and . . ." Ibid., 145.

p. 118, "Like most white . . ." Ibid.

p. 119, "We will fill . . ." Davis, *Mr. Black Labor*, 129.

p. 119, "If you refuse . . ." Ibid., 130.

p. 119, "We would have . . ." Anderson, *A. Philip Randolph*, 279.

p. 119-120, "did most emphatically . . ." Ibid.

p. 120, "PRISON IS BETTER . . ." Ibid., 280.

p. 120, "there shall be . . ." Davis, *Mr. Black Labor*, 130.

p. 122, "I'm sorry . . ." Ibid., 131.

p. 122, "weasly worded . . ." Anderson, *A. Philip Randolph*, 154.

p. 123, "If I have . . ." Davis, *Mr. Black Labor*, 132.

p. 123, "Why Bayard . . ." Ibid.

Chapter Nine: March on Washington

p. 124-125, "Who the hell . . ." Davis, *Mr. Black Labor,* 137.

p. 125, "last vestiges of . . ." Anderson, *A. Philip Randolph,* 314.

p. 128-129, "Mr. President, the . . . some problems here" David Halberstam, *The Children* (Random House: New York, 1998), 448.

p. 131, "I speak for . . ." D'Emilio, *Lost Prophet,* 349.

p. 132, "Equal Rights NOW . . ." Jervis Anderson, *Bayard Rustin: Troubles I've Seen* (New York: HarperCollins, 1997), 256.

p. 134, "Let the nation . . ." Anderson, *A. Philip Randolph,* 328.

p. 134, "It falls to . . ." Ibid., 329.

p. 134, "the man who . . ." Ibid.

p. 135, "I have a . . ." Davis, *Mr. Black Labor,* 152.

p. 135, "Free at last!" Ibid., 153.

p. 136, "I do so pledge . . ." Ibid.

p. 138, "Mr. Randolph . . ." Ibid., 155.

p. 138, "the meaning of . . ." Anderson, *A. Philip Randolph,* 328.

Chapter Ten: The Turning Point

p. 139, "the most dangerous . . ." Anderson, *A. Philip Randolph,* 108.

p. 142, "one of the best . . ." Ibid., 315.

p. 142, "In the near future . . ." Davis, *Mr. Black Labor,* 158.

p. 143, "The question is not . . ." Ibid.

p. 144, "I am sure you . . ." Anderson, *A. Philip Randolph,* 339.

p. 144, "You are the world's . . ." Ibid.

p. 144, "What we are going . . ." Anderson, *Bayard Rustin,* 314.

p. 146, "I think they . . ." Anderson, *A. Philip Randolph,* 346.

p. 146-147, "The youngsters of . . ." Davis, *Mr. Black Labor,* 161.

p. 148, "no one has stood . . ." Anderson, *A. Philip Randolph,* 348.

p. 149, "When I came along . . ." Ibid.

Bibliography

Anderson, Jervis, *A. Philip Randolph: A Biographical Portrait.* New York: Harcourt Brace Jovanovich, Inc., 1972.

————. *Bayard Rustin: Troubles I've Seen.* New York: HarperCollins, 1997.

Brisbane, Robert H. *The Black Vanguard: Origins of the Negro Social Revolution 1900-1960.* Valley Forge: Judson Press, 1970.

Broderick, Frances L. and August Meir. *Negro Protest Thought in the Twentieth Century.* Indianapolis, New York, Kansas City: The Bobbs-Merrill Company, Inc., 1965.

Davis, Daniel S. *Mr. Black Labor: The Story of A. Philip Randolph, Father of the Civil Rights Movement.* New York: E. P. Dutton & Co., Inc., 1972.

D'Emilio, John. *Lost Prophet: The Life and Times of Bayard Rustin.* New York, London, Toronto, Sydney, Singapore: Free Press, 2003.

Franklin, John Hope and Alfred A. Moss, Jr. *From Slavery to Freedom.* New York: Alfred A. Knopf, 1994.

Halberstam, David. *The Children.* New York: Random House, 1998.

Mullen, Robert W. *Blacks in America's Wars.* New York, London, Montreal, Sydney: Pathfinder, 1973.

Pfeffer, Paula F. *A Philip Randolph: Pioneer of the Civil Rights Movement.* Baton Rouge and London: Louisiana State University Press, 1990.

Record, Wilson. *Race and Radicalism: The NAACP and the Communist Party in Conflict.* Ithaca, New York: Cornell University Press, 1964.

Richardson, Ben. *Great American Negroes.* New York: Thomas Y. Crowell Company, 1945.

Web sites

A. Philip Randolph Institute
www.apri.org
Official site of the A. Philip Randolph Institute, which fights for racial equality and economic justice, working with black trade unionists to build closer alliances between African-Americans and unions.

The A. Philip Randolph Museum
www.aphiliprandolphmuseum.com
African-American labor history museum located in Chicago's Pullman District.

America on the Move
www.americanhistory.si.edu/onthemove
The Smithsonian Institution's online exhibit explores the history of American transportation, including information about the Pullman company.

The March on Washington
www.abbeville.com/civilrights/washington.asp
This site provides photographs and a narrative of the event that came to symbolize the civil rights movement.

National Civil Rights Museum
www.civilrightsmuseum.org
The official site of the museum housed in the Lorraine Motel in Memphis, where Martin Luther King Jr. was shot.

Index

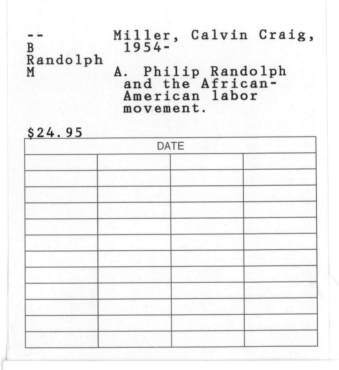